AMERICA

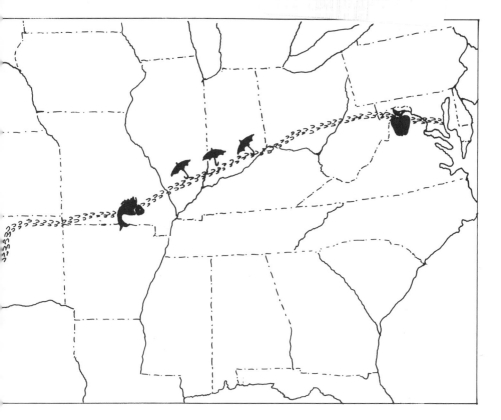

Slash and burn in the State of Rondonia, Brazil. Clearing the land for ranching and crops.
Courtesy of Randall Gingrich

RIDE ACROSS AMERICA
An Environmental Commitment

A Record Setting Journey By Horse Across the
American Environment

Written by

Lucian Spataro

University Classics. Ltd., Publishers
Athens, Ohio 45701

Published by

University Classics, Ltd.
Athens, OH 45701

Editor: Tate Baird
Science Consultant: Ray Skinner, Ph.D.
Typesetting: Samantha Cottrell
University Classics, Ltd.
Printing & Binding: Bookcrafters, Chelsea, MI

Because of our concern for the environment University Classics, Ltd.,
printed this book on recycled paper.

Library of Congress
Catalog Number 90-072061
ISBN 0-914127-44-6

Printed in the United States of America

Table of Contents

Chapter

DEDICATION

My purpose in writing this book was first and foremost to thank the many people who helped me throughout the event and those I met along the way who, like myself, are trying to effect a positive change in their own way and at their own pace. I have found they all do make a difference. I dedicate this book to these people.

More specifically, I would like to thank the horses, Sweet William, March Along, and Sea Ruler as well as my teammates, Bea and Bob Shepard and Joyce and Brad Braden whose perseverance and commitment for the duration was constant. I would also like to thank Francesca Vietor with whom I spoke everyday, and Dave Trexler and Dr. Hancock whose help early on got us through some of the rougher stretches. When I needed credibility early in the organizational phase I had help from Ted Danson, Bob Sulnick and Michael Clark.

I want to thank Mrs. Tankersley, Randall Hayes and Leslie Barclay unwaveringly supported our efforts in all cases and were always available to help us whenever and wherever we needed it. In the overall scheme of things these people were instrumental.

After the ride was over, I convinced myself to write a book, for such an undertaking I needed lots of help. I got most of the help from people who were attracted to this project for environmental reasons. For their efforts, I want to thank my publisher, Al Shuster, and those who helped me edit this book at different times: Lesley Cowling, Samrat Upadhyay, Peggy Flyntz, and Ray Skinner. And most important, I would like to thank my father, Lucian Spataro, Sr., who gave me the opportunity to have some time and space to write this book and my mother, Dorothy Spataro, who was a source of moral support and who ended up with the unenviable task of keeping my personal life in order while I was on the ride and then, later, while I was writing this book and finishing my master's degree.

Without these people and the horses, the ride and this book would not have been possible. They all, in their own way, helped bring this ride to life.

Lucian Spataro, Jr.

FOREWORD

Lucian Spataro seems to be one of those rare individuals who not only understands what might be done to improve the world, but makes opportunities to bring attention to the issues. Not only did I enjoy hearing about his journey across America, but I was amazed to discover through reading the manuscript, the true hardships and challenges Lucian faced to help us focus on our environmental responsibilities. Lucian's planned 2963 mile ride across the United States on horseback was a means of drawing attention to the destruction that we humans are inflicting on our fragile environment. He succeeded in that aim, discussing his important issues with many people along the way. Many individuals who stopped to listen did so simply because they were fascinated by Lucian and his horse, but also learned the importance of protecting our world. And now, in his book, the full story of his remarkable achievement as he brings these concerns to a far wider audience. I know you will be filled with admiration, as I was, to read the following pages.

Jane Goodall, Ph.D.
Scientific Director
The Jane Goodall Institute

PREFACE

We did it. We finished the RIDE ACROSS AMERICA at Chesapeake Beach in Maryland on October 15, 1989. I rode saltwater to saltwater--2963 miles in 150 days. In the 1800's, a wagon train would cover the distance from St. Louis to California in about 180 days. A cavalry march could cover about 30 miles per day, but only for a period of 30 days. They would then rest or change horses. More recently, in the 1970's, a young woman riding a team of three horses completed a coast to coast ride in 300 days--10 months.

By present day standards, a car traveling 60 miles an hour can cover the same distance I covered by horseback--2963 miles--in 49 hours. Our ride took 3600 hours coast to coast. Our speed was about a mile every 16 minutes. In the desert we could always see our destination, the horizon, in the distance. We had the constant knowledge that it would take two weeks and then two weeks more to reach the inevitable next horizon. But a plane flying coast to coast can cover this same distance in five and a half hours.

So you see how far technology has brought us. In the span of nearly three generations--70 years--what once took half of a year can now be done in five and a half hours. But during this same 70 year period, we laid the foundation for most of the environmental problems that we now face.

People asked us many questions along the road. But the three questions they asked most often were:

1)"Is this worth it?"
2)"Why are you doing this?"
3)"Can we save the environment?"

I answered these as best I could. And these were the kinds of answers I gave.

WHY ARE YOU DOING THIS? The simple answer to this is: we did it to draw attention to the plight of the RAINFORESTS. Someone once told me that a person cannot avoid doing what he is meant to do at the time he is meant to do it. We were meant to do this ride at this time. In 1988, the United States had experienced a frightening drought. To me, it was a sign that the destruction of rainforests in remote parts of the world was starting to affect the climate here and all over the globe. I wanted to do something about it. So did many others, especially environmental groups like the Rainforest Action Network. We began to plan the ride, with RAN as one of the sponsors. It seemed an event like this could bring attention to the issue--maybe spark a grassroots campaign.

But there were other reasons that we chose to do this particular event. I had always wanted to ride a horse across America. It would be a physical and mental challenge to me and my teammates. There was the opportunity to set a record.

Of course, once we got started, we couldn't quit. When the going got tough we persevered. We did this for the people who had backed us, helped us plan, and kept us going. But we also did it for the many people we met along the way. We had made a commitment to them. We had to finish.

IS THIS WORTH IT? As we began the event our objectives, in order of priority, were:

1) to complete the ride and establish a new record
2) to talk to as many people as we could along the way about the Rainforest issue
3) to raise as much money as possible for the Rainforest Action Network.

We felt the horses and the event would attract attention and we could then introduce people to this very important issue. It worked. We spoke to about 11,000 people personally as we rode across the United States and introduced the issue to four or five million other people through local and national articles in magazines, radio and television.

We spoke to about 75 people daily. Those 11,000 plus people heard a very strong message--we must save the rainforests now or environmental disaster will follow. Many people could not immediately relate to an issue that seemed so far away, but they could relate to our commitment.

Our example sent home a very strong message. We provided many people with an opportunity to get involved in this issue and therein lies our real success. I truly believe we convinced a large number of people to become involved in the rainforest issue and the environment.

And, finally, we brought in $84,000 for the Rainforest Action Network. This went directly to the rainforest work RAN does. RAN has over 30,000 members now and is growing very quickly. It works with more than 35 groups in 12 countries.

CAN WE SAVE THE ENVIRONMENT? It took a long time for me to find the proper answer for this question. It is something I often think about. But, finally, the answer is that we can. I firmly believe we can and that it will happen in this decade.

But, even if we can't, I believe we have a moral obligation to try. We simply do not have the right to give up. We have everything to gain by trying our best and everything to loose by not trying. For me, the challenge is to learn how I can help in this effort. I know that we, as human beings, must change our behavior--change the way we think and feel about the rest of earth and the other inhabitants of this planet. We need to understand the impact our actions have on other aspects of this ecosystem.

In the ride across America, I learned first hand about many environmental problems other than the rainforests. We kept running into them along the route. In some ways, it is more difficult to cross America on horseback in 1989 than it was in 1889. In those days, there was no need to cross highways, negotiate bridges and organize permits. In those days, too, there were not the same problems of pollution, waste and damage to the land as there are now. On the ride, I often thought about how things had gotten so out of control and what we could do to get back on track again.

It all starts with balance. How do we walk or ride a bike? We balance, using gravity and our senses. Our eyes and our ears are the primary senses that allow us to do this. If you stand on your left foot and touch your nose with your left index finger, it's still easy to keep your balance. If you do the same but close your eyes, it takes a second to get the balance you need. You have altered your senses a little.

But, if you put on your headphones and turn the music up really loud and try this, it is much more difficult. It takes your body a while longer to adjust. Some of you may not be able to adjust quickly, and may even fall over. This is because your eyes and ears work with one another to give you a sense of balance. If you alter your senses in any way your body will have problems doing what it would normally be able to do.

The environment is like your body. If one part is not able to work or is changed, the whole system is affected. The environment can often compensate, just like the body does, in the balancing act. On the other hand, if we alter the system too much, it will not be able to recover.

One summer in Arizona, a farmer had an unusually good pecan crop. He was very excited because the year before he had a very small harvest. But he also saw more birds in the orchard than in previous years and he was concerned that the birds might eat all of the immature nuts. So, whenever the farmer saw the birds, he got out his gun and shot as many as he could.

Several weeks went by and when the farmer was ready to harvest the pecans he found that the nuts were infested with insect larvae. Many of the birds the farmer had seen in the spring were feeding on adult insects. With no birds to feed on them, they had been able to lay many eggs. These soon hatched into larvae, which grew very quickly and eventually infested the whole orchard.

The farmer had not understood that the birds ate the adult insects, keeping the population down. He assumed that the birds were eating the immature nuts. The farmer did not understand that the birds really helped him keep the balance in the orchard; he did not understand the relationship between the birds and the insects. The farmer had altered a critical relationship. He upset the balance of nature in his orchard and, as a result, lost his harvest.

In other cases, the balance is not as obvious. For example, if we cut down rainforests in South America, many thousands of miles away, we do not see the impact. We are not in South America. But we can feel it. Many of the songbirds that live in the United States during the summer live in the rainforest, in the winter. If these birds have no protective place to go and no food to eat when they arrive there, they will die.

This means we will lose these beautiful creatures. As the years go by, we will hear fewer and fewer songbirds in the summer. But we will lose more than songs. Songbirds eat insects. Without them, the insect population will grow. The farmer may use pesticides to control them but some of these poisons may get into our food, or into the foodchain of animals that eat insects. So a chain of destruction started many miles away will eventually have disastrous consequences here. And the rainforests may be gone before we see those consequences.

We have realized that any change to nature can have unsuspected effects elsewhere. We feel that before we make a change, we must first study the possible outcomes. If left alone, a balance tends to evolve among all of the plants and animals. This is the BALANCE OF NATURE. As humans, we have to try to respect this balance as much as possible. And where we can't avoid changing the natural order, we should be very careful in our actions. We need to know more. Then we can think of ways to act.

1

LIFE ALONG THE SANTA ANNA RIVER

Introduction

It is about 9:30 AM and I'm sitting on my white horse, Willy, at a street corner in Los Angeles. Anaheim Stadium is off to my left, and I'm waiting to cross eight lanes of rush-hour traffic. People are honking their horns, brakes are screeching, my eyes are stinging from the gas fumes, smog, and exhaust, and it's hot and getting hotter. I'm wearing running tights, Nike 990 running shoes, a baseball cap and a small backpack. Willy has two of my shirts hanging off each side of the saddle and a water canteen and lead rope tied to the back of the saddle.

Standing on my left, on the street corner, with me is a man and his shopping cart full of clothes, cans and bottles. On my right is a young lady with a set of head phones on and a bright yellow running outfit; she is jogging in place. Behind me is an older man in a business suit, complete with a tie and a brief case. We are all waiting for the light to change. I arrived at the corner first, so I am closest to the street. I let the reins drop a bit and begin to peruse my L.A. street map. At the corner I do not push the button on the pole to provoke the light to change in my favor. Standing on that corner the three people, Willy and I wait for quite a while. No one says anything and everybody assumes I had pushed the button. I am in no hurry--I still have 3000 miles to go. After a while the man in back asks me to push the button again. There isn't a lot of room on that corner, with the shopping cart, Willy and I, the girl jogging in place, and the older gentleman all waiting for the light to change. To push the button I back Willy away from the pole so I can lean down and push the button. This move forces the guy with the shopping cart off the corner and into the street. Traffic slows to a near halt and, as I think about it now, the sight of Willy and me standing on a street corner, reading our L.A. street map waiting for the light to change, must have been startling for the morning commuters on this Friday morning. I being unfamiliar with the street system

A typical hazard in L.A., irritating smog and traffic.
Courtesy of AP/Wide World Photos

2

tried to determine how far the next bridge might be by using the designs on my bandanna as a scale for the map.

What I first noticed about L.A. traffic is that when the light changes, or just prior, people in anticipation have one foot on the gas and one foot on the brake. The second thing that catches my attention is that you never have enough time to cross eight lanes of traffic before the light changes to green in favor of the drivers. They do not look left and right to clear the pedestrian lane, but, instead, they assume it is clear because what idiot would take that long to cross eight lanes of traffic. My three friends on that corner crossed in a flash. It takes me a second longer to get moving and that second cost me. As soon as L.A. drivers see the cross light turn orange they release the brake in anticipation of the green light. My dilemma on a horse is that I am invariably caught in lane four or five as I try to cross and will be surrounded by traffic. I try trotting across but, with steel shoes on, Willy has a slippery time of it and the slower approach is much better, especially with all of the noise and commotion. A horse moving quickly across asphalt can easily get out of control. Welcome to the RIDE ACROSS AMERICA.

At 6:00 AM on the morning of May 19, 1989, as the dawn was just lighting the Pacific surf, AM Sweet William (Willy) and I rode through the sand on Huntington Beach, California, heading east on the first leg of our long journey. The Santa Anna River in years past would empty into the Pacific at this point. It no longer flows so we decided to use the dry river bed as our route through Los Angeles.

Our goal: to begin knee-deep in saltwater on the West Coast and finish four to six months later knee-deep in saltwater on the East Coast. Why? We wanted to draw attention to the various environmental problems in the world, especially the depletion of the rainforests. What better way to draw attention to the whole messy affair than to ride a horse across America?

The natural obstacles--sun, rain, wind, topography in many cases--presented fewer problems than did the man-made obstacles. Highways, cattle-guards, fences, homes, street lights, bridges, and cars and trucks by the millions were a constant source of danger and would inevitably force us to reroute ourselves or schedule night rides to avoid them. In 1989 to cross America in anything other than a car required permits, permits, and more permits. These are for beaches, roads, highways, parks, streets, towns, cities, and counties--you name it. If you go through it riding a horse, a permit is required. It took us over two years to define the route and gain all of the permits the route required. Of those 67 plus permits, California required over 30 percent, or a total of 21 permits. It seems there is not much you can do in California without a permit. To get onto the beach, be on the beach, and ride off the beach required that we obtain six permits from four different governmental groups. Our cause, the RAINFOREST, helped us break the ice with various government agencies and get some of the permits faster than usual.

To get from the beach to just west of Los Angeles was very difficult. The area is crisscrossed with numerous super highways, fences, and a mish-mash of residential areas and roads. Our first day of riding was in the dry Santa Anna river bed and along the banks of the river. Riding in the river bed and skirting it required us to go up into rush-hour traffic often on that first day. On four occasions we were forced to cross eight lanes of traffic, zipping by at 40 to 60 MPH, and numerous smaller highways.

On one occasion Willy and I were riding down a small residential street in an effort to bypass a bridge crossing. The sidewalk was very narrow and we were riding downhill. The road would meander in long curves through the neighborhood. On my right was a neck-high brick wall. As I rode into one of these long curves we came up parallel to a yard with a huge doberman and a smaller yapping terrier. I could see both dogs from my seat in the saddle. This wasn't a problem; they were only about three feet from us, but Willy could sense they were on the other side of the fence and not dangerous. Nevertheless he was still shying toward the road to our left. At that very moment a city bus pulled up on our left at a bus stop that we were nearing. Just as people were beginning to unload in front of me, I noted we had walked into a box canyon of sorts. Bus to my left, barking dogs to my right, and twenty people straight ahead all gawking and pointing at us. You would think: Still not so bad; I could simply stop and wait for the group to break up and then ride on through. Those were my intentions. I was now about ten feet from the people and stopped when I heard a petrifying noise.

Coming up from behind on the long curve, blind to this very complicated box canyon of people, buses, horses and dogs, was someone on a skateboard. The rhythm of the wheels on the board, broken every few seconds by a seam in the sidewalk, was unnerving. We had no place to go and I could tell that the board was picking up speed. Willy heard it and I heard it, but the danger didn't register with the people in front of me. They were either so accustomed to skateboards or they didn't hear this one over the barking dogs and the traffic. I couldn't move right toward the fence with the barking dogs and the bus was still a minute or two from pulling away on my left. My only chance was either to move forward or to hold our ground and hope that the board rider, when he came around the corner, could recover within about 15 feet, adjust or stop. To settle Willy down I reined him around so he could see what was coming at him. This helped, but the closer the board came to coming around that corner the more Willy backed toward the people who were now behind us and not dispersing, even though I told them to walk away quickly. I had to keep Willy on the sidewalk because in the grass on both sides of the sidewalk were sprinkler heads sticking up that could do real damage to Willy's feet, not to mention the surprise of knocking one of those off and spraying

4

water up into the air. So we were basically confined to the slippery sidewalk with the skateboard.

The skateboard came around the corner and the girl on it was going faster than I thought. I can tell you her first reaction was surprise and then immediate panic. Rather than hit us, she jumped off the board and let it go right through Willy's legs (we were standing at a slight angle--no special planning on my part) and then into the crowd of people. A boy in the crowd caught the board and gave it to the girl with whom I was now talking. This all happened so fast that, before Willy could respond in terror, the board was already through his legs and into the crowd. The whole incident took less than a minute, but I remember saying to myself that not in my wildest moments could I have dreamed up a training session which would have included all of those factors. I learned several very important lessons from that brief encounter. One that helped later in West Virginia was that, whenever possible, ride on the side of the road that gives you the most room on both sides and the longest view ahead and behind. This applies even in a slow residential area.

On several occasions as we rode along the river we met the homeless who live in the river bed under the bridges and in cardboard boxes, old cars and drainage culverts. As we rode down one trail that skirts the river, the trail would often meander down into the river bed to avoid fences that would come up against the river. In those cases Willy and I would ride down into the sandy bottom of the river and then later back up onto the edge. Riding in the river bed I came upon a small group of holes in the embankment. It looked as if some neighborhood children might have been playing war games and dug bunkers in the embankment in which to hide. The embankment was sharply steep and rose up about 30 feet to the top of the river bed. There were numerous trails coming from the top of the embankment to the entrance of these holes. There was also quite a bit of debris at the entrance of each hole. It didn't really dawn on me until I saw a shopping cart at the head of one of these trails that people, residents of L.A., were actually living in these earth caves.

On another occasion in the dry river bed I saw that the pylons supporting the bridge and anchored in the dry river bed act as a fourth wall in a three-sided cardboard house or a box. I rode through one of these encampments as the homeless were just waking up. There were some coals from some small cooking fires that were still burning from the night before, and people were standing or sitting around these fires or at the entrance of the box houses. Our trail went right up into one encampment and no one said a word as we rode through. Willy was not an enthusiastic participant in these encounters: I sensed he could feel the misery. It was a very uncomfortable contrast to ride into eight lanes of L.A. traffic with BMW's, Mercedes, car phones and convenience stores on every corner immediately after riding through an encampment of homeless people. I doubt that many people driving on those bridges know about the homeless people that live under these bridges and in this river bed. So much affluence and excess in such close proximity to extreme poverty.

California has the greatest population density of any state in the United States. One out of every nine Americans live in California. If it were considered a country, it would be one of the richest in the world.

About six miles from the beach a golf course borders the river. I could find no alternative route. Our tracks left large divots in the fairway as we cantered across to the ringing words "BALLLLLLL." It seems several golfers were teeing up for an early morning foursome. Much to their surprise, the course that morning presented a new and different hazard--a white Arabian horse and rider cantering along the fairway toward the river.

It was a very hot day and our only source of water was from the various convenience stores along the route. I would ride up, find a nice person filling up with gas, and ask them to hold Willy until I could find water. The sight of a beautiful white horse standing in a parking lot brought a lot of attention and I had no problem finding a willing helper.

Earlier that morning, just as the sun was beginning to come up, we rode by several employees who were walking in to work at a power plant. They stopped short as I rode up. I said hello. They stared, and just before they turned to go into the plant one yelled out, "Where are you riding from?" I answered, "The beach." I quickly came to learn the inevitable next question: "Where are you going?" I remember my response as though it were yesterday and we were in slow motion. I reined Willy around to face them, looked each one straight in the eye and said with as straight a face as I could muster, "New York." I'll never forget the look on their faces. Just as they were going to ask another question the whistle blew and they all ran inside. As they were running in I heard one remark, "I think he is serious." The other replied, "I saw something in the paper yesterday about this."

As I rode away I thought to myself: what an appropriate start. It was at that moment that the significance of this ride really sank in. It hit me--we were undertaking a very difficult task and we had 3000 miles yet to go. After the initial shock of this realization wore off I remember smiling to myself, patting Willy on the neck, and saying out loud, "All the way! Let's do it, just me and you." This would be the first of many conversations I would have with Willy. I had a very strange, confident feeling that we were going to make it. That pat on the neck was a pact that Willy and I made with one another and it was our own secret. It was a very warm feeling on a very chilly morning.

Three local riders, Allen Coward, Bob Smith, and Joe Wheatley, were scheduled to meet us about 12 miles up the river from the beach. Their job was to help us traverse the complicated route from the beach up into Riverside County, the point of our first fund-raiser at the Reinhold Arabian ranch. I talked to Allen on the phone several days earlier and he told me he had a route identified and that he would meet me along the river. We felt we would have no problem finding each other. It was doubtful that there would be any other horseback riders and the river route was pretty straight forward. It would be hard to miss each other unless, as I was soon to find out, we were on opposite sides of the river.

The river bed is very wide in some places--two or three football field lengths and I was riding on the west side and often had to leave the river to go over or around residential areas, bridges, and other human obstacles. So after about five hours of riding I was sure we had gone over 12 miles; by my map it was closer to 15. I was a little concerned that we might have missed each other, but I kept on riding. Willy and I rode the first leg of about 16 miles up the river bed before we actually ran into Allen, Bob and Joe. They had been riding up and down the other side of the river bed asking people if anyone had seen us. After finding no sign of us they split up and Joe ended up on my side of the river bed and eventually caught up with us from behind. We then found Bob and Allen and headed up off the river into some trails that only Allen knew. Allen Coward, L.A.'s version of "The Man from Snowy River," helped us navigate around, through, and over all of the man-made and natural obstacles that confronted us those first two days. I very quickly found out that local riders like Allen would be our best source of information, direction and guidance. In any case, L.A. was one heck of an initiation. No practice on the Tucson streets could have prepared us for what we encountered in L.A. It was good experience, however, because later in the ride we would, on numerous occasions, encounter all of these same obstacles to a greater or lesser degree. One satisfaction: For a ten-mile stretch we were traveling faster than cars along the thoroughfare to which we were riding parallel.

Allen Coward was a local rider and a blacksmith by choice. I understood from talking with Bob that Allen spent every minute in the saddle when he wasn't working. Several years back Allen was considered one of the most prominent endurance riders in the country. Allen spent many long hours in the saddle and on his motorcycle picking our route for the three days of riding. There is no question that his support and knowledge made getting through the concrete jungle both do-able and safe.

Bob Smith was a friend of Allen and the two teamed up to ride the Pacific Crest Trail from Mexico to Canada. So most weekends and many vacations you can find Allen and Bob somewhere along this trail. Because they both work for a living they ride it in stages. Joe Wheatley was a retired Navy pilot from Orange County who rode with us off and on from L.A. to the Colorado river, keeping me company for the next two weeks. We spent a lot of time together out of the saddle as well, scouting trails and locating camping spots.

It was 5:30 and Allen, Joe, Bob, and I just met Bob's wife and my teammate, Sheryl Studley, a horse masseur, about 29 miles from the ocean in a secluded canyon on one of the last old ranches in Riverside,

Allen & Melanie Coward. Joe Wheatley and Bob Smith--Horses names are Ringo. Casper. Sunshine and Cinder.

Rancho de la Sierra Vista. This ranch sits on top of a saddle that overlooks Riverside County and the area we had just ridden through and is just above Prado Dam. We were now up in the mountains and the view was spectacular. What a contrast! Our campsite seemed a million miles away from the street corner near Anaheim stadium, gas and exhaust fumes, the homeless shelters all along the river, and the white sand beach. The owners of the ranch were just getting ready to sell the property, a family ranch for more than a century, to a local developer. They told me that even last year they had seen bear and mountain lion in the orchards just below the ranch house. The weather was cool, and Allen, Bob, and Joe had just left; the team settled in for the night, and, as the sun went down, you could see the lights beginning to twinkle in the distance. That was L.A., and off to my right was New York and the east coast. I said to myself, "Don't think about the distance; just take it one step at a time." Willy was looking over the view as I was. With a piece of hay hanging from his mouth, he seemed transfixed on some object in the distance. I thought, "No, he can't be thinking about the same thing I am. He is probably wondering what in the heck we rode through today, and why."

That would not be the last time I caught Willy wondering. It was a long day and we had a 4:00 AM wake up and a 23 mile ride to the Reinhold Arabian ranch the next day. I fell asleep at 8:30 PM.

2

THE HIGH DESERT AND DEATH VALLEY

California

My interest in the environment has its roots in my youth. When I was a child in the fourth grade, I was very much interested in nature. I was introduced to the world of nature at a very young age by my parents. Even then it was very easy for me to understand that this world is operating under some kind of master plan. I was not, however, aware that this plan was a naturally balanced ecosystem.

A naturally balanced ecosystem is a group of organisms (animals and plants) within a unit that live or function together in natural balance. We are a part of this ecosystem. We are one of the organisms. When I look back my memories are of Latourette's forest, Essex' pond and Dobson Hollow. In southern Ohio we call a valley a hollow ("holler" in the colloquial).

Dobson Hollow was a very deep valley about two miles from my home. At the Eastern tip of this valley were huge rock cliffs with a red-tailed hawk nest and a clear stream and meadows down below. It seemed very few people went down into this hollow. We would spend hours and days exploring the streams, ponds and valleys. There were animals everywhere: deer, hawk, quail, largemouth bass, frogs, fireflies and turtles. I had the unique opportunity to gain an appreciation for the natural world through these sometimes aimless wanderings and exploration. I would spend many hours and sometimes days on my horse or hiking with friends through rural southern Ohio. I had a beagle named Skipper that would accompany me on many of these trips. We played a game often--I hide, you seek. I would leave home and hike into the woods, sometimes several miles. I would attempt to disguise my trail. I would then find a high vantage point--often a ridge--and watch my dog trail me through streams, over logs, from rock to rock and across wooden fences. I learned most of these tricks from watching fox and rabbits as they were being trailed. (Rabbits always return in a complete circle home.) I learned a lot about patience and persistence. We use to photograph deer from tree stands in the early morning as they were moving into the apple orchards. Through these childhood experiences I had the opportunity to become educated, fascinated and appreciative of the natural world.

I sense that this same opportunity no longer exists for children and adults alike. Or maybe it does, and many choose to simply not take advantage of the opportunity. I feel the problem runs deeper than that though. We have grown away from nature. Kids are naturally inquisitive and seek out challenge. I feel that technology, the double edged sword, has substituted computers and video games for the natural interest that many once had in nature. Without this basic understanding or exposure, both children and adults miss the very important connection. We, as a society, have isolated ourselves within our technology. We no longer feel the real cold or the rain or heat. I seriously doubt that many of us question how or where the food we eat is produced. Many of us may have only a rudimentary understanding of how it arrives on our plate. We need to rediscover nature and the fascination it held for many of us in years past.

I now understand that we, unlike other members of the ecosystem, through our behavior can dramatically alter the natural balance. And, unfortunately, we have been doing just that. This is a learned behavior; our actions and habits have been passed down to us from generation to generation. It was on this mission that I embarked--to make people aware that we can change our habits that are damaging the environment.

After we left Riverside on top of the mountain we rode through San Jacinto Valley along the Ramona Expressway and then up through Lamb Canyon and into the town of Beaumont. Riding along the north side of United States Interstate 10, we rode through San Gorgonio and Cabazon and then along a power and pipeline road through the Morongo Indian reservation to State Highway 62 into Morongo Valley. This route would eventually carry us up into the Windmill farms and then further north along State Highway 62 into Morongo Valley. For the next three days we rode east in forty-and fifty-knot winds toward the Windmill farms and State Highway 62. The winds in this valley are unrelenting and as a result the area supports the largest windmill farm in the United States. The natives often say, "This is nothing. Sometimes the wind blows so hard we change zip codes." This is not an understatement. Until you have ridden eight hours a day for several days in 50-knot winds you will not understand the significance of this statement. The Windmill farms have an amazing visual impact when you first see them stretching across the valley like a wave of white picket fences rolling from ridge to ridge. When I was about a day's ride away, they looked like small "high tech" sentinels out of a Star Wars film. Relative to the San Jacinto and San Gorgonio Mountains, the size of these windmills was hard to imagine. In the distance I could not envision the impact they would have on us as we rode through.

The next day's ride began about 5:00 AM, three hours (10 miles) from the first ridge of windmills. The wind was down enough that I could wear my cap with the bill facing forward to keep out the sun. As the wind began to pick up in the late morning, I learned to turn the bill around or lose the cap. I don't learn easily and three days into this stretch I was on my third cap. I was bound and determined to keep this last cap all the way through the windmill farms.

I was riding this stretch with Joe Wheatley, who laughed at my comment about the cap. He was wearing a cowboy hat. I knew for a fact that his hat was history. As we rode on I would look up periodically to note that Joe had his head down; so did the horses. We tried to stay low but the trail kept meandering up and, the closer we rode, the more impressed I became with the ever-increasing intensity of the wind on each successive ridge. I began to hear a faint buzz. At first I thought it was just the wind whistling, but the closer I got the more intense it became. I felt as though my eardrums were throbbing. The reverberation was rhythmic. The throbbing vibration really shook up Willy, and if the rotor on a particular windmill was moving slowly, it would periodically cast a menacing shadow across our trail. I did not see Willy look up once. I myself couldn't; the wind was so intense that I could not keep my eyes open. Fine grains of sand were swirling everywhere and both Joe and I had a difficult time keeping the horses moving forward. Both horses kept attempting to angle down the ridge. I was yelling at Joe to tell him that we needed to get off the ridge and angle off to the left. He could not hear me, although he was only about 20 feet in front of me.

The windmills were immense. The base of each windmill was actually a small house and each rotor was as long as three flagpoles. It seemed that they were not much smaller than a water tower. From a distance they seemed so insignificant, but up close rows and rows of these generators overwhelmed us. From base to base, side by side, there was a distance of about 50 yards, one-half the length of a football field. They were slightly staggered in rows, not directly side by side. I thought to myself, "As a source of energy this must be significant." ("What energy!")

Windmills used to be as common as the rural mailbox in the early part of this century. But over the next few decades electricity, oil, and gas slowly took over the energy market. Burning fossil fuel for energy in power plants is a major environmental concern and constitutes, in many areas, the largest percentage of carbon released into the atmosphere each year. Nevertheless, as we rode through the windmill farms I thought about the prevailing argument and played it over and over: an alternative source of energy for California versus "it's an eyesore" mentality.

Some say the windmill farms constitute visual pollution. But wind

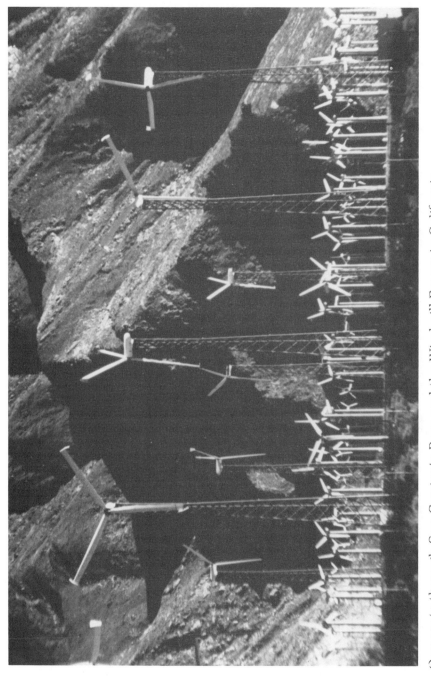

Our route through San Gorgonia Pass and the Windmill Farms in California.

Courtesy of Suzan Victoria

is a natural source of energy and by far a better source environmentally than coal. Burning fossil fuels releases large amounts of carbon dioxide into the atmosphere. This build up over time will cause a general warming of the earth's surface. It lies like a blanket over the earth; the accumulation will not allow the heat reflected off the earth's surface to escape into the atmosphere. With new technology, wind could serve as a very useful energy alternative.

Later that day we were out of the windmill farms and had bush-whacked our way up into the high desert and a town called Morongo Valley. To get up onto this plateau we had to do some climbing. In the 1920's and 30's this route had been the major spring/fall cattle route. Until just after World War II, foot-high grass grew in the area, serving as forage for large herds of cattle. Due to man's intervention, overgraz-ing, reduction in the water table, and an influx of new residents, the area no longer supports the knee-high grass and huge herds. This area is now primarily desert.

Sheryl met Joe and me on highway 62 about 5 miles from Morongo Valley. Sheryl Studley and her dog, "Patches," were the other half of our team at this stage. Sheryl is a lawyer and an endurance enthusiast who was recruited and employed by the Al-Marah Arabian Horse Ranch in Tucson--Willy's home and major sponsor of the ride--to assist in every aspect of the horse-related portion of the event. Sheryl helped coordinate water stops, scout campsites, and locate trails and routes. You would think that when riding a horse across America you could simply stop at the end of each day's ride and camp. Not so.

In the West, water and feed and your proximity to them are very important. In many places it is illegal to pull off onto the side of the road and set up a camp, so in many cases we had to identify a base camp and ferry the team back and forth at the beginning and end of each day. For example, we had a four-day base camp at a ranch east of Twenty-Nine Palms. This belonged to Larry Hobb's, a retired rodeo cowboy who let us stay free of charge. The first day we camped there we rode out of Joshua Tree, through Twenty-Nine Palms and right into camp at Larry Hobb's ranch, about 27 miles. The next day we rode out of camp and about 20 miles east of Larry's ranch into a region just south of the Death Valley. There are no gas stations, stores, water, or any of the other necessities we needed to sustain the team. So at the end of each day we marked a spot on the side of the road with a pile of rocks or a big orange marker, and Sheryl picked Willy and me up and trailered us back to Larry's ranch. On the following morning we would load Willy up and drive out into the desert. We found our marker from the afternoon before and began riding from that point. On the fourth morning we loaded up the whole team and drove to the drop-off point. Sheryl left Willy and me and then drove east 60 or 80 miles to a predetermined base camp. She then set up camp and at noon came back to pick up Willy and me. We were covering about 20 miles per day at that point, so in this case we would be west of camp about 40 miles. We would ride 40, 60 or sometimes 80 miles to each base camp, trailering back and forth each evening and morning and then 40, 60 or 80 miles past each base camp and then jump to the next base camp. In this manner we leapfrogged our way across the desert. In the East, our camps moved every two or three days, as available campsites were more numerous.

These were logistics I had planned for in Tucson (where I had been living before the ride), but I never actually had a chance to work through them until we got on the road. In planning the event I knew that logistics and our route would play a very important role, so I spent a lot of time ascertaining our route and alternate routes. There were many items for which I could not plan, so Sheryl and I spent the first two weeks working the bugs out of this system, trying to make it as efficient and safe as possible. Taking down the heavy corrals each morning and loading them onto the trailer initially took about 20 minutes. By the time we got to Larry's ranch, we had a system that took less than 5 minutes. Some things were now falling into place!

Sheryl and I were living in very cramped living quarters and had known each other less than three weeks. It was what you could call a pre-arranged marriage of sorts. This was as much a people event as it was a horse or endurance event. With this in mind, Sheryl and I initially spent a lot of time laying down the rules, personal do's and don'ts; this planning and talking was very important because we were basically living together, whether we were compatible or not. The fact that we were very busy trying to establish a routine and a rhythm and that the event was so physically draining was in our favor. We did not have the time or the energy to think much about any differences of opinion. Our focus was very short term--the next 10 miles, next water stop, campsite. This focus got us through the first couple of weeks; I call it our honeymoon without many major personality clashes.

During these first three weeks we spoke with Al-Marah daily about the horse and our route. Our training in Tucson was, in some ways, very appropriate and, in other ways, not useful. I spent a lot of time in Tucson training in traffic and this was very helpful in California. Once I left Riverside, however, my traffic training was not much help. I didn't see a major city until Albuquerque, some 700 miles or about 5 weeks later. The traffic work we did helped in some of the smaller towns, but I think what we did in Tucson was overkill. By the time we hit Albuquerque a string of semi's passing us within two feet would not cause Willy to as much as lift an eyebrow. I think he was suffering from vehicular overload. Often on the highway or smaller two-lanes the rhythm of the cars swooshing by had a hypnotic effect on both Willy and me. I soon learned that those were some of the most dangerous times in our ride.

We were having one problem after another and solving most, but one problem continued to baffle us. Willy was going through his first set of shoes faster than we had envisioned. We were 15 days into the ride and he needed new shoes. We knew this situation was not going to change and that this was a major hurdle that we needed to overcome. A horse's hooves grow slowly and a new set of shoes will usually last two or three months or longer, dependent to a great extent on mileage. To secure a set of shoes to the hoof you drive nails into the hoof wall. Typically the hooves will grow out, and, when you pull the old shoes to reset or change them, the new hoof wall will be sufficient to find room for new nail holes. In our case we needed to change the shoes faster than the hoof wall normally grows out. For the first two sets of shoes this was no problem. But for any shoes thereafter we would not have enough new growth to secure the shoes with new nail-holes. We knew this might be a problem so our veterinarian, Dr. Hancock, located an endurance company in Sante Fe, New Mexico, called Easy Boot. This company is in the business of providing rubber boots as shoes for horses in endurance events. These boots are high-impact rubber boots with clamps that fit over the horses steel shoes. You clamp these rubber boots on over the hooves and they last over 800 miles, or 4 weeks, three times what the steel shoes alone were lasting. This system is very helpful because it allows the hooves to grow out naturally and the steel shoes can serve as a back-up in the event that a horse would throw an Easy Boot. In this case we would still have the steel shoes to ride on that day, and then I would simply take off the other three boots so that the horse could walk evenly on all four steel shoes. We had a little pow-wow with our team veterinarian and made the decision to continue riding into Arizona with Steel Shoes and then fit Willy in Flagstaff with Easy Boots. A strategic decision. As I look back, without them we would not have gotten any farther than Texas. It was also a pleasure to meet Neal Glass (the man who holds the patent for these revolutionary "horse boots") and his wife, Lucille, who personally flew into Flagstaff to fit Willy with an exact pair of boots.

As we continued working the bugs out of the event and making progress across the desert, it was becoming more apparent each day that we did not have enough team support on the road and that we needed more help. Between Sheryl and myself we were barely able to attend to the horse chores, riding, trailering, media work, and administrative functions for the ride. We needed more help. Unknown to me, Mrs. Bazy Tankersley, owner of Al-Marah and the first person to support the ride, had come to this conclusion months earlier during our training sessions in Tucson. She had the name of a man and his wife who might be willing to join the team.

The ride through the high desert and down into the Colorado River basin is both very bleak and very beautiful. Temperatures vary on a daily basis more than 50 degrees. Our route, along State Highway 62, was about 75 miles south of Death Valley. This is the lowest point in America, almost 300 feet below sea level. There are ten lakes along this route, all of which are dry. The Colorado River aqueduct carries water from the Colorado river to Riverside, California. For a portion of the trip the aqueduct was parallel to our route. It was a very tempting potential source of water, but we were unable to take advantage as it is fenced on both sides. Our ride in the morning would begin in about 50 degree weather and would end that same day in 110 plus temperatures. This was early summer in what many call the most unforgiving environment in America.

On Memorial day, hundreds of miles from any town, a continuous string of cars coming from L.A. passed Willy and me on the way to the Colorado River for Memorial Day. Many people stopped to inquire about our presence in the desert so many miles from cities or towns. I told them about our event and said that I would see them at the river in June. Before we could reach the river I saw many of these people returning two days later. They waved and wished us luck.

Illustration of Sheryl's helping Willy cool his hooves in the desert.
Courtesy of Rosemary Renteria and Angie Wood

Time moves very slowly in the desert and it is very quiet. Waves of heat shimmer off of the asphalt and sand. As it becomes hotter you begin to work yourself into a trance, and it is often very difficult to stay awake. Willy and I covered those 250-plus desert miles often on "automatic." The miles just seemed to drift away, broken up by necessary water stops and a car every 20 or 30 minutes. Sheryl would drive out into the desert with buckets of water. We used this water to drink and stand in. The temperature on the asphalt was over 200 degrees. The high temperature, in combination with the friction of the steel shoes striking asphalt, was a serious concern. To avoid damaging Willy's feet and tendons from the extreme heat buildup, we would get Willy to stand in water buckets. The water would dissipate the heat. If it was still early morning, very quickly steam would come rolling out of the buckets. The water in the first buckets would soon become so hot that it would scald you if you were to stick your hand in. As soon as the water became this hot we would add new cool water and eventually get the temperature of Willy's feet and ankles down. At these water stops I would douse myself with water. Wearing a long sleeve shirt and bandanna over my head kept me relatively cool.

Art Parker, Gene Wagner, Larry Hobbs in front of The Hitchin Post, Twenty Nine Palms, California.
Courtesy of Suzan Victoria

We worked our way across the desert in this manner, consuming on any one day over 250 gallons of water among crew, rider, and horse. Our stay in the high desert was made much easier by Al Cox, Gene Wagner and Art Parker, our friends at the Hitching Post, Feed and Tack store in Twenty-Nine Palms. They donated hay and grain, entertained us as we debated the merits of real horses (Quarterhorses versus Arabians), drove supplies out to us in the desert, provided us with a place to stay and discussed with us every inch of road from Twenty-Nine Palms to the Colorado River.

Best of all, they introduced us to Larry Hobbs. Larry at the age of 73 rides four hours every day. He spent thirty years of his life as a rodeo cowboy, during which he was known as the "Cyclone Kid." If Allen Coward was L.A.'s version of the "Man from Snowy River," then watching Larry was like watching the "Man from Snowy River" time warp and span two generations. During the 1950's, Larry ran a ranch that stretched from Skyline Boulevard to Half Moon Bay on the Northern California coast. This ranch was owned by an ex-governor of California, James Rolph, Jr., and Larry spent many hours telling stories about the ranch and the area just north of Monterey Bay.

Larry Hobbs and his horse Bob.
Courtesy of Suzan Victoria

Larry was tall, lanky, with bright twinkling eyes, sunbaked and as close to a caricature of the Marlboro man as you'd find. Not surprisingly, we soon found that Larry was as well known for his prowess with women as he was for his rodeo riding. Said Larry about his thirteen wives: "They all wanted a cowboy. When they got me they didn't know what to do with me."

We learned from Larry that Guinea hens make the best watch dogs. Said Larry, "The coyotes can't get close with a Guinea hen in the yard." Before we left Larry took us to his favorite restaurant, an old inn in the high desert that is still a favorite watering hole for Hollywood's old guard. Under Larry's strict orders and confidence I've been sworn to secrecy and am unable to reveal the whereabouts of this beautiful hide-away. I am sorry.

Finally, on June 3rd, we crossed the Colorado River and rode into Parker, Arizona. The couple Mrs. Tankersly found for us, Brad and Joyce Braden, joined the team along with another trailer and truck. Brad brought a second Al-Marah horse, AM March Along, with him to keep Willy company and provide a riding companion for me on some of the lonelier days. Our team is now two horses, one dog, and four people on the road.

We made some strategic decisions and changes during the California segment and one of the most important was to add Brad and Joyce Braden to the ride. Mrs. Tankersley met Brad at an Arabian event several months before and spoke to him about our event. Brad's comment at the time was that it would sure be fun to go along on that ride. Mrs. Tankersley called Brad at his home in Texas as we were approaching the Arizona border and asked him and Joyce if they would like to work with us. Four days later we met them in Flagstaff and brought them down to our base camp along the river. Brad and Joyce were there to help us in the many horse-related activities and also to act as a second or third opinion when talking with our team veterinarian over the phone.

Brad and Joyce are well known Arabian trainers and ranch managers who have been involved in the Arabian industry for over 35 years. Brad spent several years in the early 1930's on border patrol, riding 20-30 miles each day along one or more stretches of the United States and Mexico border. We needed a person on the team with that kind of experience, someone who could act as a experienced second opinion and was familiar with horse-related illness and injury as a result of day-in and day-out riding. I also often needed a second opinion on terrain. My first inclination was to always take the shortest and straightest path. With Brad's knowledge of terrain and its effect on the team, horse, and riders, we were often able to pick a more advantageous route.

We had three other team members who did not travel the road with us but worked closely from their locations in Arizona and San Francisco to keep us informed and prepared. Brad and Dr. Hancock would

DEATH VALLEY

ROUTE ⋙⋙⋙⋙

C A L I F O R N I A

(DRY LAKE)

DEVILS PLAYGROUND

BRISTOL LAKE (DRY)

CADIZ LAKE (DRY)

DANBY L. (DRY)

LOS ANGELES

ANAHEIM RIVERSIDE BEAUMONT

JOSHUA TREE

TWENTYNINE PALMS

RIVER AQUEDUCT

HUNTINGTON BEACH

PALM SPRINGS

Larry Hobbs Ranch

COLORADO

CHOCOLATE MOUNTAIN

SALTON SEA

Our route through the desert south of Death Valley.
Courtesy of Rosemary Renteria and Angie Wood

speak by phone on a regular basis about the horses and their condition. Dave Trexler, the General manager of Al-Marah Arabians in Tucson, worked closely with Dr. Hancock and Brad on horse requirements and vehicle logistics. And Francesca Vietor in San Francisco was our media and fund-raising coordinator. She worked for our other major sponsor, the Rainforest Action Network, and worked closely with the team to coordinate all of the media events and interviews along the road.

At the end of the ride that day (June 3rd) Willy and I rode into the Colorado River to cool off as weekend boaters from L.A. zoomed by. Little did I know, as I stood in the cool Colorado river, of the things that would happen to me and Willy as we continued on our journey. One state down, we still had a long desert ride ahead to the mountains in northern Arizona, then the painted desert and the Indian reservation, plus a long hot stretch in New Mexico, Texas and Oklahoma. We had survived one state but we were not yet in the land of milk and honey. The thrill of crossing the Colorado was short-lived as I thought of the desert ahead, the vast expanses in Texas and the hot humid ride in the Midwest.

3

THE PAINTED DESERT & THE INDIAN RESERVATION

Arizona

On June 4, 1989, the 17th day of the ride, the new team was moving along the Colorado River on the Arizona side. The elevation was sea level. We were on State Route 95 heading north for Interstate 40, northern Arizona and the city of Flagstaff, elevation 7,000 feet. Leaving Flagstaff, our ride would take us up through the Navajo/Hopi indian reservation and the towns of Ganada and Window Rock. We would then cross the Arizona/New Mexico border and drop down into Gallup, New Mexico. From there, we planned to take Interstate 40 through Albuquerque, New Mexico, and on into Texas.

This was one hot stretch. I consumed about 3 gallons of water per day and didn't even use the bathroom. The horses were drinking about 10 buckets of water per day as well. I told myself many years ago that when I decided to get married I would take my fiancee on a cross country trip in an old car without air conditioning in the summer, coast to coast. If we could make it across the United States in good spirits and still be good friends and still be in love when we hit the coast, then we could probably remain married through almost anything. I've changed my mind; I'll just take her on a horseback ride through the California and Arizona deserts.

In this stretch we were so thirsty, we thought about water all the time. The sensation of thirst was central to our very existence. In 1821 the scientist Rullier said: "Thirst is universally held to be one of the pleasures of life. The sensation cannot be ignored, and if water be lacking, thirst comes to dominate our thoughts and behavior; it drives us to the utmost endeavor and achievement . . . or to the depths of despair and degradation."

The human body is 65 percent water by weight. Under normal

conditions we must replace 1.5 quarts per day of water to survive. People can go without food for many weeks. People can go without water for only a few days, or sometimes only hours under certain desert conditions.

This was one hot stretch. We got drowsy and began to daydream often. Willy and I both fell into a trance and cars that went by often

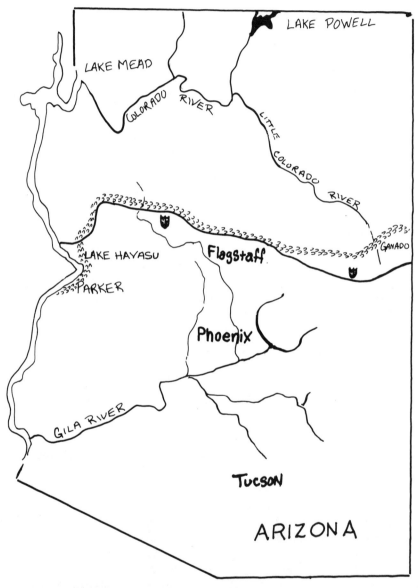

Our route through Central and Northern Arizona.
Courtesy of Rosemary Renteria and Angie Wood

had a hypnotic effect on us both. They seemed to be timed by the desert gateman. The rhythm of these cars whooshing by, together with the steady rocking of our walk, quickly began to play tricks on our minds. One of the hardest tasks was to remain alert. In these situations I would often let my mind wander, and this gave me an opportunity to do a little experiment.

Over a four-day period I wrote down in my journal all of my thoughts, no matter how brief. On June 9th, in a one-hour period, I thought about the following:

* Ride logistics, food, water, campsites, fuel, newspaper interviews and a TV interview we did.
* old girlfriends
* high school
* Cold water
* the OCEAN and scuba diving
* how to fix my computer to communicate off of a phone line
* the RAINFOREST
* how little I think about my business
* mirages and how they appear
* my family and what they are doing
* Willy and how tired he must be
* what Willy must be thinking about
* how tired I am
* pessimism and why so many people are pessimistic
* optimism, are these two traits innate or learned?
* an empty coke bottle: in the United States it represents garbage, in the movie THE GODS MUST BE CRAZY it represents an opportunity and a host of new ideas
* how important real friends are
* all of the animals that live in the sand on the side of the road and that their world is so small, so limited, yet so dangerous. The road is a very dangerous boundary. Our world is so large. I came to the conclusion that it is all relative.
* how bad we must smell, no shower in three days
* the temperature in the trailer last night was 109 degrees
* why the desert buzzes
* the only animals I saw during the two hours were a buzzard and a butterfly
* we still have 2000 plus miles left to go
* I must be crazy to run a test like this; it keeps me alert.
* swimming in college on the swim team
* justifying my independence
* how sore my tail is, and if numb means it's getting better or worse.
* why am I doing this, really why?

These were the thoughts I could recall and document during a one-hour period. It is difficult to believe that you can think about so many unrelated thoughts in one hour. I found that it was very important to let my mind wander and relax. Documenting this was very difficult. On the California, Arizona, New Mexico segment WATER and activities related to water were predominant in my thoughts. This ride was as much a mental event as it was a physical event. The mental aspect may have been much more important. Not focusing, I let my mind relax. I found early on that if I worked both my mind and my body I would quickly drain myself of energy. I needed that energy physically during and at the end of each day and to keep up my motivation and enthusiasm and that of the other team members. Along this stretch members of the support team began to feel the strain of the ride, and we hit the first wall in the marathon.

On the evening of June 12th, actually early in the morning on June 13th at 1:00 AM, Joyce and I took Sheryl to the hospital. She was nauseous and faint. We found out at the hospital that she was severely dehydrated and as a result was suffering from borderline heat stroke, actually heat prostration or severe heat exhaustion. She was hallucinating and her fluid level was down so much that it took 4 liters of fluids and three hours in the hospital to bring her around. The intern on duty told us that this was a very serious matter, that these kinds of situations have a way of turning for the worse quickly, and that we were very smart for responding as we did. He also mentioned that if we had to move on it was very important that we keep Sheryl out of the sun and under observation. The temperature in the trailer that afternoon: 123 degrees.

Sheryl was not from a desert climate and was not familiar with many of the ordinary common-sense precautions that people who work and play in the sun normally take. For instance, wearing hats, bandannas and long sleeve shirts, seeking shade and drinking water, are some of the simple things we can do to keep our bodies properly hydrated. As a result, working in the sun twelve hours a day and then trying to sleep at night in temperatures that would minimally exceed 105 degrees took a toll on Sheryl. Precautions I assumed Sheryl knew were not as apparent to her. At the hospital I found out from Joyce that earlier that day, in the afternoon, Sheryl, after completing her horse chores, decided to combine some swimming and relaxing with a good book. The Colorado river for a stretch near our camp was about waist deep. This gave Sheryl a chance to swim and then sit in the river and read.

Sheryl spent over three hours sitting in the river with only her head and the book sticking out of the water. With no hat, the reflection off of the water served to magnify the intense radiation and turned her fair skin and freckles into a very bright beet red. From her shoulders up, Sheryl was bright red, like a lobster dipped in boiling water. She said she was not feeling well. I said nothing. Sitting in that cool river all afternoon misled Sheryl into believing that she was, in fact, cool; meanwhile the heat and the river were drawing water out of her body and literally cooking her brain. Needless to say, Sheryl spent the next two days under observation, in the trailer or in the shade. I shudder to think what might have happened if we were in a more remote camp.

The extreme heat, uncomfortable living conditions, 3:00 AM wake-up calls and intense working conditions began to show. As a result we were often working with very little sleep--mechanically. The pace and the work were very draining. We had to keep our motivation up and concentrate to avoid making mistakes. A miscalculation or misunderstanding could cost us many hours of riding time or, in some cases, put us in a very dangerous situation.

Shortcuts, bridges, cattle-guards, fences, mountains all had to be calculated into each day's ride along with stops for water. The strain began to take its toll, on Sheryl first. She began to become less attentive as I began to note early signs of fatigue set in. For example, back at Larry Hobb's ranch in California the water used by Larry and the ranch hands came from a scalding hot underground spring on the ranch. The water is pumped at 4:00 PM each evening and then sits in cooling tanks overnight, the cool evening air helps to bring the water temperature down so people can shower and cook with it the next morning and all day. Larry had warned us about this. One evening Sheryl, giving Willy a bath, used up all of the water. This drained the cooling tanks, causing them to pump over night. The next morning Larry was as bright red as a lobster in his early morning shower. But this burn was due to the heat of anger, not the hot desert sun.

Just after our trip to the hospital with Sheryl she asked us what year it was, if the Colorado river was man-made or natural and argued we were riding in the wrong direction as Las Vegas was south of Arizona. I told her that it was 1989, the Colorado was natural and that all of those gamblers would have problems placing bets in Spanish.

I knew that the worse was yet to come and that the heat in the painted desert, plus the long hours and confined living conditions, would only intensify our problems. Under this kind of day-in and day-out duress we needed a strong team. We did not have the energy or the time to carry anyone. Emotionally, physically, and mentally, everyone had to pull his or her own weight and, thus far, Sheryl wasn't able to do this on a consistent basis. I kept hoping that she would grow into the ride and become more responsible as the ride wore on. This was not happening. As her physical strength began to wane, so did her commitment to the event. There was also a conflict brewing between Brad and Sheryl on issues related to Willy. Too many chiefs and not enough Indians.

There was only room on this ride for one horse expert and Brad, the polite cowboy that he was, would often go out of his way in an effort to diffuse the growing tension and not confront Sheryl directly. As a result the much needed day-to-day consensus related to Willy's feeding schedule, water requirements, type of feed, mileage per day, and bathing--were very difficult to reach. I knew as the ride wore on that this tension would only grow worse and might eventually erupt and ultimately jeopardize the event. While we were up in northern Arizona at the Al-Marah Hat Ranch the growing tension was apparent to others as well including Al-Marah ranch management, the sponsors of our ride. This in combination with some of the physical requirements of the ride caused us all to review the staffing for the event and ultimately the consensus was to reassign Sheryl to other activities within the Al-Marah organization. Sheryl left the ride in Northern Arizona and after a short rest she moved down to southern Arizona to begin working at the Al-Marah ranch in Tucson.

On June 11 Brad, riding March Along, and I riding Willy crossed the London Bridge. This bridge was shipped over from London, England, piece by piece, bricks, lamp posts, etc., all in original condition. It was reconstructed here in Lake Havusu City, Arizona, as a tourist attraction.

On June 12 it was hot at 11:00 AM. We were on State Route 95 heading north to Interstate 40 east. A man in a Cadillac passed us. The driver braked, made a U-turn, pulled up next to us and rolled down his window. "What are you doing on that horse?" the man asked. "I'm riding him to New York City to raise money for the Rainforest," I replied.

The man motioned me closer. As I leaned over in the saddle to look inside his car he flipped a switch and the outside temperature was displayed on his dashboard. "You damn fool, it's 117 degrees out there." The man's electric window came up as he made another U-turn and sped on down the highway.

We made the front page of the local paper that evening. The response the next day along the highway was more favorable. Many stopped to chat and ask us how they could help.

Each evening in camp we set up a table with pledge forms and information on the Rainforest. We had brochures in the saddle pack and I passed these out along the way as well. People who read the articles in the local papers or saw us along the road stopped by our camp in the evening and talked. I was usually in bed by 7:00 PM.

As we worked our way through the mountains of northern Arizona, the temperature was much cooler at an elevation of 3500 feet. We were riding along Interstate 40. In this area we could ride off the interstate parallel to the fenceline that borders this route. We were picking our way along this fenceline through volcanic rock, juniper and cactus when Willy began acting very strange. His ears jumped at attention and his neck stretched out, nose on the ground. We were just approaching a very large juniper tree with branches that hung down to the ground. Willy was snorting, flaring his nostrils and sucking in great amounts of air. We were obviously up-wind of something.

As we continued to inch forward I heard low snarls. Willy also heard these snarls, and we both had the same idea--get the heck out of there!

Same idea, different directions. As I made my turn to the right,

Willy made his turn to the left. Just then several coyotes exploded from the juniper dragging a very large carcass. Now about four feet from the tree, we went all ways at once. I lost a stirrup, but managed to stay in the saddle. The coyotes didn't seem willing to give up any ground to Willy and me and stood over their meal. We left them with the carcass, retracing our steps along the fenceline.

Illustration of Willy and Lucian meeting the coyote clan in Northern Arizona.
Courtesy of Rosemary Renteria and Angie Wood

During this stretch across northern Arizona, we spent ten days off and on at a ranch, resting and riding. The ranch belonged to Bazy Tankersley. The Hat Ranch resides on 125,000 acres of Forest Service land with elk, bear, antelope, cows and horses.

It was a welcome break from the heat in southern Arizona. The ranch is still very much unchanged from the late 1800's, but now they do have a phone and a generator. This ranch and other ranches like it form part of the Colorado River watershed. Small tributary streams in these and other mountains combine as they meet one another flowing south into the Colorado River drainage basin. The Colorado River basin is a major source of water for all of Arizona, southern California and northern Mexico. It supplies water to other rivers and streams and underground lakes and aquifers in this region.

Central Arizona Project (CAP) bringing water from the Colorado River to Tucson.
Courtesy of Don B. Stevenson

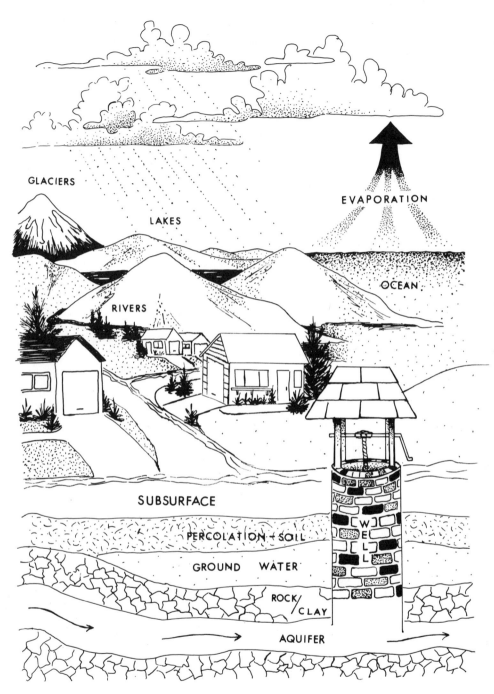

Illustration of the water cycle--rain water collects from the mountains and residential areas and drains into streams, lakes and underground aquifers. It then evaporates or is brought to the surface by wells and the cycle continues.

Courtesy of Rosemary Renteria and Angie Wood

31

When it rains the Colorado River drainage basin can be compared to the streets in a city, where water runs down the driveway and into the street. There it combines with the water from all of the other neighborhood driveways and flows down the street to meet with the water from another street. It then flows into a larger stream that might travel to a river or lake outside of town. In a similar fashion the Colorado river takes water from northern Arizona, Utah, Nevada and New Mexico, a very large area of mountains, streams and lakes, and feeds the southwestern United States, Mexico and the Sea of Cortez. This water is instrumental to these areas, and the people and economies in these areas have grown to depend on it.

We are draining the river dry, however, and this is causing several problems. Some of the consequences are political, affecting the relationship we have with our neighbor, Mexico. Some affect the growth and success of cities and towns and ultimately our ability to remain in the desert and continue to live and prosper there. In 1934 Arizona and California were at odds with one another over Colorado River water and the rights of each state to use it. In 1944 this was further complicated by an agreement between the United States and Mexico mandating that the United States provide Mexico with 500,000 acre feet of water each year from this river. An acre foot of water is the amount of water that covers one acre, one foot deep. This is a lot of water, and right now we are having problems meeting our requirement. The United States is draining the river and also polluting it, so we are giving Mexico less and poorer quality water. The quality of the Colorado River water is very important for a number of reasons.

As the water from the Colorado flows south toward Mexico it becomes saltier; that is to say, the concentration of salt becomes higher in the remaining water. There is a higher concentration of salt and other material in the river the farther south it flows. What causes this? Primarily water consumption by people. We remove water from the river and we leave the salt and chemicals in the water that remains. We also construct dams and reservoirs along the river, causing the salt and chemicals to collect.

Clean drinking water does not exceed 500 parts per million (PPM) of dissolved solutes. Water used for growing crops and irrigation is typically 800-1,000 PPM. Plants are not salt tolerant and will die if you use saline or salty water on them. Sea water has about 35,000 PPM of dissolved solutes so you could not use sea water on plants. The Colorado is naturally, without interference from man, 400 PPM, which means that at its origin (way up in the watershed) the water is still clean and we can drink it. As the water travels down into the drainage basin and then south toward Mexico we begin to drain off water for irrigation and human consumption and we add chemicals to the river from run-off from the agricultural fields and sewage from cities and towns along the river. All of this, in combination with a reduction in water, causes the salinity to go up. So in some cases we cannot use the water for drinking or growing plants without processing or cleaning it first.

Salinity is a major concern as the Colorado River flows into northern Mexico and the Sea of Cortez, often known as the Gulf of California. This saltwater body needs fresh water; it is like a very large lake and its only source of fresh water are some small rivers and streams in Mexico. From the north, however, there is only one source of fresh water and that is the Colorado river. Fresh water flowing into the northern Baja mixes with the salt water and this lowers the salinity in the Sea of Cortez. Many of the saltwater fish, plants and animals that live in this area have adapted to this salinity level. By causing the salinity level of the Colorado to increase we are increasing the concentration in the Sea of Cortez as well, and many of the plants and animals that live there are dying as a result.

There is not as much fresh water from the river emptying into the Sea and this makes the whole northern Baja saltier. This affect staggers the food chain and has a significant impact on plants and animals that rely on these organisms that are dying off. The whales are no longer able to breed in the northern Sea of Cortez. They stay farther south where they feed on plant and animal life that can no longer live in the northern region on this sea.

The Mexican fishing industry in this area is also adversely affected. As you can see our excessive consumption has a dramatic and very complicated impact on animals, plants, and human communities in two different countries.

We often take water for granted. We do not understand that it is finite in its natural state and that, we will eventually run out of it. Once we use water it is no longer naturally clean and we must then clean it either naturally (100's of years) or mechanically through a man-made process.

One evening in northern Arizona I wrote in my journal: "The sun is just going down in vivid red and orange, and here I sit in the midst of all of this natural beauty typing in my journal on my Toshiba lap-top computer. Technology, the double-edged sword. High tech in the middle of the desert. All I can hear are the keys as I type."

I also typed in my journal the question of the day: "What happens when someone creates a clone, a patent on lab mice clones and clinical frog clones? Taking this concept one step further, we create human clones. Are these clones owned by the creator as they are with lab mice and frogs, or are they human? Genetic engineering. Do we have the mental capacity to keep pace morally with our technology and manage it as quickly as we create it?"

At this point in the ride we have covered 800 miles and are now 27 percent of the way across the United States. We have been on the road for 60 days. During this same time we have lost over 300,000 acres of rainforest and several hundred species of unknown and undocumented plants and animals. Lost forever.

The Arizona Department of Transportation did not give us permits for a stretch of Interstate 40 from Flagstaff to the New Mexico border. This forced us to route our ride up through northeastern Arizona and the Navajo/Hopi indian reservation.

In looking back, I'm glad we had the opportunity to ride through the "Res," as they say in this area. Physically, this area is much like it was a 100 years ago. The country is beautiful, bleak, empty and desolate. No electricity or running water and very few towns. A crossroad might have a gas station and a convenience store. To do any shopping for groceries or clothes the Navajo must often travel 200 miles or more one way. They do this monthly.

On the reservation our camps were very primitive. Because we had hay and feed in our trucks and water in our storage tanks, we became a midnight attraction for many of the wild horses and cows in the vicinity. Each evening we were visited by very aggressive cows and horses, which made Willy and March Along very nervous at night. These wild horses would snort and kick outside our trucks attempting to get in. Each evening we would alternate standing guard over our camp and take turns chasing the wild stock off. This would go on all night until daybreak. I spoke to the Indians about this and they said that the following week they were going to have a round-up. All of the stray cows and horses that did not have brands would be shot and sent to Flagstaff. There just wasn't enough water and forage to go around that summer.

On the reservation, water rationing was a problem so we often went without showers, using the available water for drinking and cooking only. The horses came first and the human team members second. On the reservation, in Ganada, Arizona, each evening for seven days we made a trip to the fire station to fill up our water tanks and make our phone calls. There was only one phone and we were limited to 75 gallons of water in the morning and 75 gallons in the evening. That supplied two horses and three people with just enough water. The people on the reservation did this every day of the summer.

By contrast, on an average day, an American family of four cooking, washing clothes and dishes, bathing and flushing the toilet can consume 500 gallons of water. Bathrooms account for most of the water used in a home each day, the largest amount of this used for flushing the toilet. We realized, on the reservation, that you can save quite a lot of water through these easy conservation methods. On our ride we used all of these ideas every day. We had to. Water in the desert is very precious. We could only carry so much water and we often had to ration it.

In the Southwest water is considered gold and is the miracle re-source. Water can transform the desert into a garden and a dusty crossroad into a thriving community. Although water uses and usage vary across the country, in the Southwest agriculture, farming and ranching are still the primary consumers of water. Close behind that

Here is a breakdown of water consumption:

ACTIVITY	NORMAL (No. of gallons)	CONSERVATION (No. of gallons)
Shower	Running water(25)	Wet down, turn off water--soap up, rinse off (5)
Brushing Teeth	Running water(10)	Turn water on and off (1)
Bath	Normal (36)	Shower (4) or fill tub to a minimal level (10)
Shaving	Running water(20)	Fill the sink (1)
Dish Washing	Running water(30)	Fill the sink (5)
Dish Washing	Full cycle (30)	Short cycle by machine (7)
Toilet	Normal (7)	Conservation (4)

WATER CONSERVATION

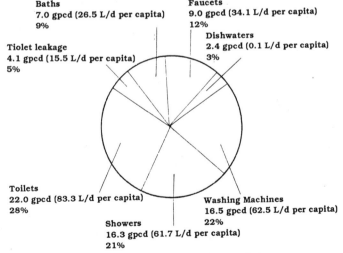

Baths
7.0 gpcd (26.5 L/d per capita)
9%

Faucets
9.0 gpcd (34.1 L/d per capita)
12%

Dishwaters
2.4 gpcd (0.1 L/d per capita)
3%

Tiolet leakage
4.1 gpcd (15.5 L/d per capita)
5%

Toilets
22.0 gpcd (83.3 L/d per capita)
28%

Washing Machines
16.5 gpcd (62.5 L/d per capita)
22%

Showers
16.3 gpcd (61.7 L/d per capita)
21%

Total = 77.3 gpcd (292.6 L/d per capita)

Source: Residential Water Consevation Projects-Summary Report.
Brown and Caldwell (June 1984)

Where water is consumed in a household daily.
Courtesy of Rosemary Renteria and Angie Wood

are municipal and industrial uses for cities, towns and companies. In Arizona, 60 percent of the water is used for agriculture, 20 percent for cities and towns, and 20 percent for mining and industry.

In the Southwest most of the water for drinking and agriculture comes from wells and reservoirs. Underground water is very clean, but surface water, water from rivers and reservoirs, is often polluted or saline. So we in the Southwest continue to pump clean water out of the ground to drink and use. We are very quickly depleting the supply of water in the ground, and the water table (the level of water in the ground) is being reduced at a much faster rate than it is being replenished.

In general it takes about 4,000 gallons of water to produce $1 of agricultural product. The mining industry takes 58 gallons of water to produce $1 of product. Petroleum refineries consume 9 gallons of water to produce $1 of product. The electronics industry takes 2 gallons of water to produce $1 of finished product. So as you can see, farms use 2000 times the amount of water that the electronics industry uses to produce the same $1 of finished product. Farms are a very inefficient use of water in the desert, as you might have guessed already. It is feasible and cost effective for a farmer to keep producing crops in the desert only as long as water remains inexpensive.

The emphasis on farming in this area does not make good sense from a business or environmental standpoint. In using this water, we must gain the most economical return on this environmental asset or resource. With that in mind, it would make more sense to use water in the desert for homes, business and industry. We could use much less water and it would last for a longer period of time if we would push for water-efficient projects. In the future we might even reach a point, in our efforts to conserve, where our consumption may equal the desert's ability to replenish the groundwater table. We need to encourage businesses that are water efficient, i.e., electronics, recreation, tourism, cities, towns. If we continue to produce farm crops we are going to drain the water bank and leave nothing. How do we make this switch? We raise the price of water dramatically. This will price the heavy water users out of the market and will force us all to conserve now for the future. We should also pass legislation that taxes heavy water users now. This will encourage people to conserve water the way the Navajos do, and as we did, out of necessity, when traveling through this area.

About one-half of the way through the Navajo reservation, riding along a lonely stretch of road, I happened upon a 16-year-old girl who was walking home. I had not seen a car in over an hour and I was more than a 20-hour ride from the nearest town. I saw no towns or houses on the horizon. I asked her where she lived and she pointed at the horizon to a ridge of low mountains at least 40 miles way. We were walking along together at about the same pace so I got off and put the duffle bag she was carrying on Willy. It was heavier than Willy's saddle, at least 70 lbs, but much lighter than I and very heavy for a 16-year-old girl to be carrying in the heat of the day on a long hike.

As we walked along I found out that her name was Tammy and she had been in Flagstaff in a drug rehabilitation program. The program was over and she was free to go home for a few days. The problem was getting there; she had no ride and her mother had no car. She wanted to see her grandmother, who lived on the reservation, because Tammy felt that the addiction she had for drugs was still with her. Her grandmother told her that she would work with the medicine man to help rid her of these spirits. Tammy spoke with a speech impediment which, she explained, was a result of a drug overdose.

She used to run cross country until she got involved in drugs. She said she wanted to start running again when her body and mind were no longer "dreaming of drugs." I told her I, too, used to run cross country in high school. We walked together for about 10 miles. Then she turned to me and said that over the next ridge was her trail and that she must turn off the road as her trail veers east.

As we topped the ridge I expected to see a road or two-lane truck trail, but nothing marked the spot. I asked again with some doubt and what must have been an incredulous look on my face: "Are you sure this is where you get off?" It was empty, simply desert and mountains, no sign of people. She replied: "Yes." She had no water so I filled up her plastic jug with the rest of mine. I knew Brad would be by within the next two hours. I could now tell time by the sun and my shadow. She gave me some fry bread, waved good-bye and walked off into the desert. Within minutes I could no longer see her.

I continued to have strange experiences on the reservation. On July 2, I was riding along a stretch of dirt road with no sign of human activity in sight. I knew from the maps that we were about 15 miles from the nearest crossroad. This dirt road was a shortcut that I had spotted several days before, but I had not scouted out the route as I usually did. So we were riding blind. I had told Brad to meet me at a specific location on the other side of this mountain at a specific time.

As we climbed into the mountains there were many small roads branching off; I kept to the most worn of these roads hoping that we would eventually end up back on the main road in time to meet Brad. From my vantage point I could see about 50 miles in every direction, and our road was dropping down into a large valley. As we got to the bottom I heard a shrill whinny to our left. Having already encountered wild cattle and horses, I didn't want another encounter in the middle of nowhere. Also, I didn't want to canter on down the road, because that would draw more attention and possibly cause the group of horses to chase us. When horses meet one another they often kick and bite to establish a pecking order. This is usually okay when all of the horses are not encumbered with a saddle and rider and are free to maneuver, but, in this case, Willy was at a disadvantage, and I didn't want him or me to get hurt in this introduction.

Illustration of wild horses on the Navojo/Hopi Indian Reservation in Northern Arizona.
Courtesy of Molly Zehr Palmer

One minute later I saw a dust storm rolling toward us off the ridge. It was a group of horses, and they were running full tilt directly at us. Willy was prancing in circles and I was doing everything I could do to hold him back, not knowing if he wanted to run or fight. I was determined to stand our ground because I knew we would tire too easily in an all-out sprint. It was late in the day and we were 18 miles into a 24 mile day, temperature 104. We were tired. I thought we might bluff them if we stood our ground. They were now about a football field away and going full out, six of them, all different colors. Willy was all over the place and I had to keep him prancing in circles to keep him in place. The lead horse was red and had a screaming whinny. There was a white horse running next to him, stride for stride, but this horse was quiet.

Just as they were closing in on us Willy suddenly stopped prancing, turned to face the oncoming horses, planted his feet wide apart and stood very still and very steady, not shaking but very tense. The leading red horse stopped and snorted. The other horses stopped in a cloud of dust milling behind the lead horse. This whole encounter took just about 3 minutes. It was a standoff. Bluffing confidence, I clicked a knee into Willy to square him off to the lead red horse. We were about 20 feet apart, close enough for the red horse to reel and kick us. Not seeing any brands, halters or ropes, on these horses, I thought maybe they were real wild horses. The red horse was flaring his nostrils and weaving his head up and down, snaking it around as if he were trying to get a sniff on us. This went on for about 30 seconds; the wild horses did all of the stamping and snorting. I did not want to add an unknown variable to this drama, so I said nothing. About a minute went by in the standoff, with the other five horses milling around behind the red horse. Willy and I stood our ground becoming more and more confident by the second.

Then it dawned on me that the red horse was blind. He couldn't see us. The white horse was his lead. How did he run so smoothly across the desert toward us? I waved my hand and he didn't follow my movement. He did, however, react to my voice. He nipped the white horse next to him and they trotted off in rhythm, leading the other four horses with them. For the next hour they shadowed us at a distance. Then they just disappeared into a Juniper forest. I looked down at Willy's shoulders and they were covered with white lather. I was drenched in sweat.

A three-legged horse: mirage or reality? On the same day during the end of that ride I was on a two-lane road riding toward the spot where Brad and I had agreed to meet. There were fences on both sides of the road, and red clay, low sage, and cactus for miles to my left and right. I saw a small hut up on the mountain to my right. It was still very far away but I could see some people moving around it and some horses in front. To my left there were some cattle moving, maybe a mile out in the desert. As I rode down this road I saw the people to my right saddle up--two people and three horses. They seemed to be leading one horse.

As these persons began riding toward the road, I thought that I would have to trot to meet them as they were crossing the road. They were still very far away and moving faster than we were. When they got to the road they were about half a mile ahead of us. They disappeared and then reappeared on the other side of the road, now to my left, riding toward the cattle. Not unusual; they were probably going over to herd the cattle to another part of the range and went under the road through a drainage tunnel or culvert. As I got closer and they continued to move farther to my left into the open range, I noticed the third horse was not on a lead and was limping as though he were lame. The closer I got, the more evident the limp. When they were about 100 yards to my left and heading straight off my left shoulder, I noticed the last horse only had three legs. This third horse would stop and then trot and then hop as it tried to keep up with the other two.

I stopped Willy to watch this very strange procession move on after the cattle. It seemed as if the second rider might be the son and the first rider the father. The son kept waiting for the three-legged horse to catch up. By the time they got to the cattle they were very far away from us and they simply brought the cattle into a very tight circle and kept riding right up into the mountains, the third horse dragging behind on three legs. I was disturbed by the sight and I thought, "How cruel, bringing a three-legged horse on a trail ride."

When I passed this story on to the other people on the team that evening, they thought I had been out in the sun too long. I swore up and down that I had seen a three-legged horse that day. Nobody believed me. Some day I am going to go back up onto that reservation and find that hut and that rancher and ask him if he has a horse with three legs.

Just as we began crossing the Indian reservation I got a note from my brother, John. It was a song from the seventies by a group called America and it fit my situation.

On the first part of the journey I was looking at all the life
There were plants and birds and rocks and things
There was sand and hills and rain
The first thing I met was a flower and a buzzard and a sky with no clouds, the heat was hot and the ground was dry but the air was full of sound
CHORUS
I've been through the desert on a horse with no name
It felt good to be out of the rain
In the desert you can't remember your name cause there ain't no one for to give you no name--La la la la la la la la la la la la
After two days in the desert sun my skin began to turn red
After three days in the desert fun I was looking at a river bed and

the story you told of a river that flows made me sad to think it was dead

CHORUS

I've been through the desert on a horse with no name
It felt good to be out of the rain
In the desert you can't remember your name cause there ain't no one for to give you no name--La la la la la la la la la la la la
After nine days I let the horse run free cause the desert had turned to sea
There were plants and birds and rocks and things
There was sand and hills and rain
The ocean is a desert with its life underground and a perfect disguise above under the cities there lies a heart made of ground but the humans will give no love

CHORUS

I've been through the desert on a horse with no name
It felt good to be out of the rain
In the desert you can't remember your name 'cause there ain't no one for to give you no name--La la la la la la la la la la la la

I would hum that song non-stop. It makes a reference to cities and towns buried by humans with no love for the ground they build upon. The desert, our environment, is filled with plants and birds and rocks and things, but we see none of it. As the song opens up we see it all: we are looking at all of the life around us and we get caught up in this and lose ourselves, our names. Later we bury nature and no longer see it. This song was my constant companion.

4

THE PREACHER AND THE BLUE HOLE

New Mexico and Texas

We crossed into New Mexico on July 4th. Country star Waylon Jennings was playing in concert on the reservation in Window Rock, Arizona, just west of the Arizona/New Mexico border. I rode by the concert hall on our way through town. I would have liked to attend but the concert was sold out five days after tickets went on sale. I thought that this was an interesting place to play in concert on the Fourth of July.

Crossing into New Mexico was significant for a number of reasons. We were just shy of being one-third of the way across the United States and we were now in another time zone. We added one hour as we crossed into New Mexico. You might think that at the pace we were traveling one hour would not make a difference, but it did. It made a significant difference in the early morning. We could now set the clock one hour later and still be on the road before daybreak. It took us several days to adjust to the new schedule. By far the most significant aspect of New Mexico was that we added two more members to our team.

When we reached Gallup, New Mexico, we stayed at a KOA campground. After our ride that afternoon I spent about two hours talking with the KOA manager and his wife about our event and the rainforests. They were so interested in our event that they offered to let us stay for three days "on the house." We gave them a T-Shirt and a video on the event.

July 6th was a rest day. I spent the day working with Brad on our route through Gallup on old highway 66 and then farther along Interstate 40. Later that day I spoke with local city officials and the local paper about our ride and the issue. I did two radio interviews and a television interview which we saw on the 6:00 PM news. This was very good publicity for the manager of the KOA campground and, as a result, he offered to allow us to stay longer if need be. We now had room, time, and plenty of water, enough that we could give both horses a warm water bath. What a contrast. Only two days before on the reservation, we had just enough water to cook with and to keep the horses going.

Joyce and Brad gave both horses a long hot bath and even put some conditioner in their manes and tails. This exercise attracted quite a bit of attention in the campground from both children and adults and, when Brad started lunging Willy, a crowd gathered to watch. Lunging a horse means you tie a 30-foot long rope to the horse's halter and let him travel in circles first at a walk and then a trot and then at a canter. You control the horse with verbal cues. Brad was extremely good at this. Willy would canter and stop on Brad's command, then turn and go in the opposite direction. Willy was on Brad's lunge line and Joyce had March Along on the other, going in opposite directions right next to each other. Both horses were clean and had their tails up and heads forward, prancing like show horses. After we were done and the crowd dispersed, a man walked up to Brad and introduced himself. They spoke for a while and then invited us over to his trailer for a snack and a cold drink.

The man was Bob Shepard. He and his wife, Bea, are originally from Connecticut. As a result of some very good business opportunities, Bob had the chance to retire very early from his business and had been on the road with Bea traveling all around the United States for more than a year. At the time we met, they were in Gallup and headed east along the same route we were traveling. They lived literally in a high-tech house on wheels. I was very much impressed with the video and camera equipment, the computers and the satellite dish which was on top of the Winnebago. An idea popped into my mind.

We had an agreement with Channel 9 News in Tucson to send back video and TV spots along the way and they would show our location to the people in Tucson each week on the Thursday evening weather report. The evening news would show on the weather map a horse and rider crossing the United States. Our progress each week would be closely followed in Tucson by my friends and family, and people at Al-Marah. Every once in a while I could convince a local TV station along the route to send in its piece to the Tucson station and they would show that along with the piece on the weather map. This generated quite a bit of interest in Tucson. The TV station asked me if they could get some video each week along with our location and a phone interview. If I could not get actual TV footage from local stations along the way, the station would accept the video. We did not have any video equipment with us so they were a little disappointed.

After I saw Bob's equipment that evening, I told him the story about the TV station. He offered to do a little video for us the next morning. We later found that Bob and Bea were actually professional camera people.

The following evening as we sat in the Shepard's house on wheels, Bob showed us the whole day's ride on video. It was amazingly well done and very creative. He got up in the early morning and did the early part of the video in the dark with lights and then caught us off and on throughout the day as well. I promptly asked him if we could send this piece to Tucson. He said "no problem" and offered to travel with us to document the event on film. He didn't simply mean for the next couple of days--he meant for the rest of the trip. And we still had three months to go.

I promptly said, "Fine, no problem. Glad to have you aboard."

Bob and Bea were in their mid 40's and looked like each other physically and acted like one another as well. Their personalities were as perfect a mesh as I have ever seen in a couple, with the exception of maybe Joyce and Brad. I have now found, on this trip, examples, although differently matched, two ideally linked couples. I couldn't help but think that I might, along the way, be able to pick up some tips from both couples that might put my love life back on track.

While we were riding on the reservation in Northern Arizona, Bob and Bea were on the reservation as well, visiting with several of the tribe's artists in some of the more remote areas of the reservation. The couple had developed a fascination with the Indian Kachina dolls and spent quite a bit of time and money looking for originals. I was impressed when they showed me one that sold for over $2500. The detail was incredibly intricate and ornate and they had several in the Winnebago that they would pull out now and then to show us, and then very carefully pack them away again.

When I think of Bob and Bea, I will always think of Kachina dolls. We became my very good friends over the course of this ride as I began to bounce problems and ideas off of them.

Bob became involved in working with Brad on the route logistics and Bea, with Bob, assumed responsibility for setting up interviews along the road and clearing our route through the small and larger towns we would encounter. Bob also began working more and more with Francesca of the Rainforest Action Network to coordinate our route and other logistics while I was on the horse each day. This all took a lot of pressure off Brad and me. Now I could concentrate on riding and overall logistics and Brad could concentrate on horse-related activities and vehicle logistics and problems. So we quickly integrated Bob and Bea into the team as we all easily assumed slightly more specific tasks.

Just outside and east of Gallup, New Mexico, is a small row of houses and farms. As I rode through this area I saw on two occasions an open-air church. These looked more like a podium covered with a sheet metal roof in a cathedral arch and rows and rows of chairs facing the podium. I thought, "How uncomfortable in the winter." It didn't rain often, but still these churches, if you can call them that, must be there for only impromptu teachings and speakers in the summer, spring and fall. As I rode past the facilities, I really wanted to see a congregation sitting in the chairs and someone speaking at the podium.

It was early on a Monday morning, so I was really amazed when around the next corner I heard a minister. As we rounded the bend in the road, the minister said, "These kids nowadays have no common sense, no horse sense." Just as he said the words, "horse sense," Willy let out a loud and shrill whinny. Willy is not vocal as horses go, and prior to that and, to this day, Willy has not ever repeated that performance. That was the one and only time I ever heard him nicker, other than maybe a snort of recognition at March Along. The sermon stopped and the whole congregation turned around and stared. We were only about 75 feet from the outdoor church. I was laughing hysterically and pointing at Willy and shrugging my shoulders as if to say I didn't ask him to comment. The timing was impeccable. I looked around and saw no other horses anywhere that might make him react with a whinny. I just chalked it up to the fact that Willy overheard the preacher and simply disagreed with his comment.

We moved our camp to Grants, New Mexico, about half way between Gallup and Albuquerque. This area of New Mexico is desolate but beautiful, with immense red rock bluffs overlooking the desert that straddled both sides of the highway. We had an exceedingly beautiful section to ride through that afternoon and the area would make a spectacular backdrop for a picture. Louise Serpa, a photographer from Santa Fe, came down and shot several rolls in the mountains along the highway. For these shots I rode in cowboy boots and wore Brad's cowboy hat--not my usual attire--but we needed some props for these shots. After these shots I quickly changed back into my Nike shoes and running outfit.

If you have to do any walking out in the desert you don't want to be encumbered with cowboy boots. My choice of attire was most appropriate for this ride. I know because, for example, the one time Brad got his truck stuck in the desert back in Arizona he walked about one mile in his cowboy boots and had blisters for a week. If for any reason I wanted to do any hiking or climbing and was leading Willy, I had to do it in shoes I could maneuver in. But for the sake of these pictures the cowboy attire was most appropriate.

Louise Serpa was a well known western rodeo photographer who has pictures in galleries all around the United States I don't think she would have shot it any other way; along with this, Al-Marah wanted some of the shots to be western as well. We thought if the shots came out we might be able to use them in a poster of some sort and sell these with other Rainforest t-shirts along the road and at various fund-raisers, such as the one coming up in Santa Fe at Leslie Barclay's ranch.

The fund-raiser in Santa Fe at Leslie Barclay's place was our first one since Flagstaff, three weeks before. Leslie called her place Rabbit Junction, and, from our standpoint, the road that meanders up to Leslie's house was a rabbit trail, fine for most trucks and cars but

On the interstate in New Mexico.
Courtesy of Louise Serpa, X9 Ranch, Vail, AZ

46

much too small for our three large rigs and trailers. We should have known better, but the road continued to narrow as we made our way up to the house. The combined total length of all three of our rigs was over 200 feet. So 200 feet from Leslie's front door the caravan stopped. Luckily, Leslie had a circular drive. One hour later, with some maneuvering and more than a little damage to Leslie's newly landscaped front yard, we managed to get this caravan all turned around and headed back down to an area just off the main road and next to a guesthouse. On this ride nothing came easy.

Leslie was on the board of advisors for the ride. She was instrumental in our success thus far and had a real interest in this event. For this fund-raiser she sent out more than 200 invitations. We had about 120 people turn out for dinner and to watch a video on the ride. We spent two days in Santa Fe doing interviews and resting. Then we trailered back down into Albuquerque and back to our base camp along the route.

Our caravan on the way to Rabbit Junction.
Courtesy of Bob and Bea Shepard

Leslie and her husband, Ruckie, own the Barclay Rutgers Art Gallery, in Santa Fe, and it was nice to see Louise Serpa's photography there. I was really looking forward to seeing how the shots along the route were going to come out. We said our good-byes in Santa Fe and left early the next morning for Albuquerque.

In Albuquerque we rode through town at midnight along old State Route 66. We found out at the end of the ride that day that the third shift police captain was a rider and had told his officers that he wanted to be sure we had no trouble as we rode through town. Police cars shadowed us the whole way, clearing the alleys and streets well in advance of our arrival. It was great.

Later, however, we were stopped seven times in a one-hour stretch along the highway just east of Albuquerque. Officers from three different precincts and two different agencies were astounded when they found out we had a permit to ride along the interstate in New Mexico. A permit like this had never been issued prior to our ride. I finally began taping my permit to the saddle like a license plate. When the next two officers stopped us, I simply pointed to my license plate. They detained us for a short time, then let us go on our way. I was concerned that we were not maintaining the minimum speed required. That became the joke.

Francesca and Bob had set up an interview session with the local media in Albuquerque at the Rio Grande Nature Center. This natural park, with very few trails, was enough to confuse half the media people who tried to show up. We thought it would be a good idea to have our press conference at this beautiful location which would make a good setting for a photo shoot. The press conference produced three newspaper interviews, plus spots on two TV stations and one radio station. Several other media groups got lost trying to find the park, and those that did, could not follow our directions or find the right trail. We learned a very important lesson: make it easy and simple for the media to attend. They are very busy and do not have a lot of time to search for the locations for an interview, let alone do one.

Needless to say, all of our future interviews would be held in well-known locations. After this last interview session Bob scheduled a Rotary meeting for us to attend so I could get a chance to speak with about 300 local businessmen. That was a full day and then back to camp and bed. We had a long drive the next day to our starting point, about 75 miles outside of town and then the team would break camp and head for Santa Rosa, New Mexico.

Riding into Santa Rosa I crossed the Pecos River. In 1540 that river had quite a lot of water flowing through it and the small plaque on the two lane bridge said:

"Francisco Coronado camped here for four days in 1540. He built a wooden bridge across the Pecos river: Coronado was looking for Quivera and its cities of gold. Coronado went on into Kansas from here," Brad loves history and wrote all of this down. We took a picture of him and me standing next to this plaque with Willy.

Santa Rosa is a small town of about 2500 people with several RV parks and quite a few hotels and restaurants. Because of its distance from Albuquerque, it receives quite a bit of business from truck drivers along the interstate. Santa Rosa also has a Rotary Club which Bob attended and spoke to the members about the ride and the rainforest issue. As a result, word spread quickly and we had several visitors at the campground and along the route.

Santa Rosa is also the home of the "Blue Hole." I could not resist. I had been riding past these signs for several days and I was intrigued. A scuba diving spot in the middle of this desert-like area! After our ride that afternoon Bob and Bea and I went to the "Blue Hole." We were all very much impressed with the large spring: thousands of gallons of cold, clear water poured out of this hole in the ground every second.

There were several scuba divers in the spring. I was told the bottom was about 90 feet down, but that there was a false bottom at about 60 feet. I wanted to take a look and felt confident that I could get down about 60 feet. As a scuba instructor in previous years I had done quite a bit of free diving--I could hold my breath for over two minutes and dive down to 60 feet.

What I did, many times, with my new students to train them in the art of "buddy breathing" was, on their first couple of dives, I would let them swim around a bit, 15 or 20 minutes in about 40 or 50 feet of water. Then I would dive in with no tanks and free dive down to one of them and ask for air. This would always catch them by surprise, and it would take them a second or so to respond to my need for air and to begin buddy breathing. I could buddy breathe till I saw another student maybe 30 or 40 feet away and then I would leave and swim over to that student. I could spend 10 or 12 minutes under water without tanks, jumping from student to student. It was great practice for me and not dangerous at all. If I couldn't reach a student, I would simply go for the surface. For the students it was great training because when I did reach them, I was desperately in need of air. Under true conditions, they learned what it means to buddy breathe.

In this case, I thought I could dive down to the false bottom at about 60 feet, find a diver, ask for air, and stick around long enough to check out the bottom.

I always get a kick out of seeing the expression on a person's face when he sees me swim up in 60 feet of water with no tank and ask for air. My only concern was that several years prior, during an emergency rescue, I suffered a debilitating over-pressurization injury to my inner ear. In essence, I blew my eardrum and fractured a bone in the round window of my inner ear. As a result, I lost 30 percent of my hearing in my right ear. This accident cut my diving career short. Since then I have been diving only twice, both times against the recommendations of my doctor. Both times in warm shallow water and with tanks.

But it had been over three years since my last dive and over six years since the injury. This reasoning brought me to the conclusion that I should be able to do a deep free dive with no problem and that my ear was probably strong enough to take it.

At about 20 feet down I stopped to equalize and blew my eardrum. Cold water rushed into my inner ear and caused me to lose my sense of balance, and, as a result, I become very nauseous. With this loss of balance came a loss of direction, also.

In situations like these, some divers can't even find the surface. When you have tanks on, even with the extreme pain, you are taught to watch your bubbles and you know where the surface is. In a free dive you don't have this same opportunity, and the pain is simply excruciating.

Luckily, having been in this situation before, I did not loose my wits, got it under control and found the surface.

Bob an Bea took me straight to a local doctor, who cleaned some of the blood out of my ear. The doctor described the rupture as a medium-size tear and suggested I take some antibiotics and stay out of the water until the tear heals. As his contribution to the ride, the doctor did not charge us for the visit or the antibiotics. I was in pain and very nauseous. We went back to camp and I went to bed at about 2:00 PM for a 3:30 AM wake up call the next morning. What I thought would be a way to unwind really backfired. Live and learn!

I spent the next days riding and recovering from my run-in at the "Blue Hole." We were making very good time and were all in pretty good spirits. We were now in a town called Tumcumcari, New Mexico. Joyce and Bea had been in the town earlier to do some shopping and had found several good stores for antiques. Joyce bought an old typewriter for her journal and Bea bought some groceries. I was going into town myself to deliver some mail and do some shopping for food. I also wanted to find a good restaurant for all of us to eat at later that evening. I dropped off the mail and went on to the local Safeway.

While standing at the copy machine, five cents a copy, a local 25-year-old, more than a little drunk, walked up and said to me, "We don't like your kind around here." I stood there a second and asked myself what it was that he didn't like. My clothes didn't fit the bill locally and my bright orange bike hat did stand out. It must be the running tights. I was still pretty burned out from the ride that day and still wearing my riding clothes, pretty grimy looking. I wasn't talking to anyone or doing any interviews and was low profile so I didn't see any need to change. I was just trying to blend in, obviously not succeeding.

I quickly realized that the young man and his friend were bound and determined to make this confrontation a point. Now I'm not a real big person and don't weigh much. But I am quick. In this case, my agility put me at somewhat of an advantage. The young man and his friend were obviously drunk and barely able to stand up.

I turned slowly from the copy machine and walked up as close as I could get to the man and asked him what, specifically, it was that he didn't like. That confused him. At this point several people stopped to watch. Just as he was getting ready to respond I pushed him with both hands on the chest. He lost his balance, fell backward and over the mop display at the head of this particular aisle. His companion watched and said nothing. The manager of the store came over to apologize to me and then escorted both men out of the store.

I finished making the copies and, as I was leaving, asked one of the check-out clerks at the register whether she could recommend any good restaurants. "Are you carrying a knife or a gun?" she asked. "Neither," I said. "That leaves only the Holiday Inn and the motel next door. After that incident you'd best be carrying one around here. Word spreads fast."

Late that evening we all went to the Holiday Inn and played pool. Brad and Joyce and Bob and Bea did some dancing and I watched. On day sixty-seven, July 24th, as I was riding through Amarillo, Texas, a film crew came out in the early morning to film Willy and me for the evening news. The reporter asked me several questions about the ride and our purpose. At the end of the interview he asked the most important question: "What impact does deforestation in the rainforest have on Amarillo, Texas, and this area?"

This question reflects what people in the area were all asking themselves as we were riding through, and epitomizes the attitude of many in the Midwest. I wanted my answer to bring home the importance of the rainforest and strike a connection in a way to which the people in this area could relate. I thought: Climate; this area is known for farming and ranching.

I answered, "Deforestation and loss of rainforests has an impact on global climate. This includes the panhandle of Texas as well as the Midwest and other areas of the United States " That struck home. People in this area need rain and they need an appropriate climate in which to grow crops and ranch.

5

THE CALM BEFORE THE STORM AND THE UNSEEN CURRENTS WITHIN

Oklahoma

I call Oklahoma "the calm before the storm" because some of our toughest times were yet to come. We were now on what we thought was the final turn, headed into what we thought was the final stretch.

We had ridden through the Texas panhandle on Interstate 40. We were planning to cut through Oklahoma in a straight line on secondary roads, then north again along Old Route 66 up into Joplin, Missouri. We were halfway now, and, in an event like this, the final stretch is the last 1000 miles. The final turn is the halfway point.

On August 9th, we rode into Cordell, Oklahoma, a town of about 5000 residents, and probably had our most enjoyable stay yet. Cordell's mayor, Floyd Craig, met us at the courthouse, which is the focal point of the town square, and presented us with a check from the City of Cordell. He also offered to let us stay at the city park free-of-charge for as long as we wanted. We had people from Cordell stop in all day long and each evening to wish us well and to talk about grain and hay prices, the economy and--very knowledgeably--about the rainforest.

We shared the limelight that week with the groundbreaking ceremony for Cordell's newest industry, a chicken-processing plant. It seems that a Cordell resident had been in the East at a party with friends when the host mentioned he was looking for a new site in the Midwest to process chicken. The resident had promoted Cordell as a great location, and one desperately in need of new business. After two years of lobbying, Cordell now had a chicken-processing plant that would employ about 150 workers. We were invited to the groundbreaking ceremony as guests of the city of Cordell.

I rode early that morning, about 3:00 AM, so I could attend the groundbreaking. All of the city and state officials were there. As Mayor Craig introduced them, they each had a second to make a comment. This took about one hour. Then the city presented the Cordell resident who made all of this happen with an official "Thank You" from the City of Cordell.

Mayor Floyd Craig giving March Along and Lucian a check from the city of Cordell.
Courtesy of Bob and Bea Shepard

I wanted to see first-hand how this plant operated. I love chicken and have been known to sit and eat 20-plus thighs at one sitting. On the road, I would often eat 15 or more pieces of chicken at one meal. Brad used to say I eat like an Indian, that is to say, I don't eat for days and then I will consume a whole buffalo, or, in this case, a cargo of chickens. My real interest, however, wasn't in the food but in the facility; I've been in and out of a lot of manufacturing plants, and I wanted to see how technical this facility would be, whether they used robots or automated equipment. I was impressed--this was a fully automated facility. They can process and package several thousand chickens per hour. Most of the 150 people employed by the plant were administrative or shipping personnel. It wasn't as I had envisioned it at all. People come in contact with chicken parts only twice, at the onset and at the end of the process.

At the end of the tour, everyone re-assembled in the lobby and had an opportunity to do a taste test. After going through the plant, my appetite plummeted and I did not eat my usual 15-plus pieces. The tour did not seem to affect the appetites of the others as much, and everyone dived in. Just as Bob, Bea and I were getting ready to leave, Mayor Craig mentioned to the crowd that Cordell was also proud to be hosting another group of celebrities, the RIDE ACROSS AMERICA team, and asked us to speak. I spoke briefly about the ride and the rainforest, but for some strange and unusual reason I felt uncomfortable speaking about the rainforest in a chicken-processing plant. Maybe it was bad Karma from the thousands of chickens that go through there daily.

We had a choice to make in Cordell: we could stop and rest up a week or two or bring in a third horse. Our dilemma was two-fold: I was trying to finish in six months or less, and, to do this, we needed to average just over 20 miles per day, every day. We also needed to stay on a relatively tight schedule to make it to the various fund-raisers, speaking engagements, and publicity events that RAN had set up along the route. I also did not want to finish the ride in a snow storm on the East Coast. So our schedule was very important, and we needed to maintain our average each day. The pace was tough on everybody but mostly on the horses, to whom we had our first obligation.

At this point in the ride, we had about 1600 miles under our collective saddle. 1400 of those were on Sweet William and the balance on March-Along. To keep up the pace, Mrs. Tankersley, Dr. Hancock, and Brad made a decision to bring in another Arabian horse to work in tandem with March-Along on into the East Coast. So Mrs. Tankersley sent an AL-MARAH trailer out from Tucson with a driver and a fresh horse.

John Winnicki drove all night and all day and got into Cordell, Oklahoma, with Sea Ruler on August 10th. The last time I had seen John was back in Flagstaff, so his encouragement was well-received. The last time I had seen AM Sea Ruler was in April, three months before. We made the switch, sending Sweet William back to Tucson for a much-needed and deserved rest. We than began to alternate Sea Ruler and March-Along every other day and sometimes on the same day. I was now averaging about 27 miles per day with 1300 miles left to go.

Sea Ruler was a six-year-old endurance horse. He had competed in several endurance events before the ride. During our training in Tucson, I worked all three horses all the way up to the day we left for the West Coast to begin the event. Al-Marah made the decision to use Sweet William as the lead-off horse just two weeks before the start of the event. Our intent was to take Sweet William as far as possible, and hopefully, all the way.

Back in Tucson three months before, Sea Ruler was personally my first choice as lead-off horse. He was a bit flighty though and much younger and less mature than either Willy or March Along. Before I began working Sea Ruler, his previous rider told me that he would shy at almost anything--stationary or moving--and sometimes even at his own shadow. During this time, I worked Ruler in Tucson on the city streets and trails; not once did he shy.

I was a little disappointed when Al-Marah chose Sweet William over Ruler, but I was learning quickly in the horse business. In athletics, the athlete does what the coach says and that works best. It becomes a problem when the athlete tries to play coach or questions the coach; then--things fall apart. Al-Marah was the coach and trainer, and I was the rider. This ride was no different than, say, for example, the Kentucky Derby; the jockey rides and the trainer tells the jockey how to take the horse out that day, slow or fast, and how far to take him. The jockey's job is to listen to the trainer and to keep on riding. When I got back from a day of riding, Brad and I would discuss any problems I might have had with the horse or with the route, and Brad would make some mental notes or scribble something in his notepad. Each day we would make necessary adjustments.

The rider's feedback is essential in the decision-making process. As the rider, I have the real feel for how a horse is moving that day--if he is ready to move out or is lagging; how his gait is; whether he is tight or loose; and what his attitude is, which is probably the most important factor. Like people in such an event, a horse will develop an attitude either as a result of his being tired or bored or his feed--you name it. We had to keep these horses motivated as we did the people. The ultimate decisions, however, lie with the trainer. In this case, the trainer, the team at Al-Marah and Brad chose Sweet William as the lead-off horse.

Sea Ruler was a taller, leaner, almost gangly-looking Arab standing next to Willy, who had the perfect and typical Arab physique. Sea Ruler was like a little kid--he was very playful and tried often to get March Along upset or bothered, just for the fun of it. He had a tremendous amount of energy and was always ready to pick up the pace, often even on that last mile at the end of a 20-mile day.

In contrast, AM March Along was a twelve-year-old grey gelding, a ranch horse for several years. He was the oldest horse of the three, and I rode him in situations where I needed a dependable, steady mount, usually through city streets and in small towns. I began our training in Tucson with March Along, then began working Sea Ruler and, finally, Sweet William. March, as Joyce would call him, had a more philosophical, unruffled attitude. So did Sweet William. Unlike those two, Sea Ruler could turn on a dime and would often catch me napping.

AM Sweet William was our lead-off horse and the horse that did it all. He was an eight-year-old grey gelding as well, who, before this trip, was considered an accomplished Hunter Jumper, winning several awards and events. He was a quiet horse, steady through rain, heat, mountains, water and a hundred small towns and cities. He did not have the emotional surges in energy that Sea Ruler had or the stoic outlook that March had; his attitude was steady and relentlessly persevering. I describe it as "He went after it" slow and steady, reeling in the miles: 30 miles to Riverside, 400 to Arizona, 800 to New Mexico, 1200 to Texas, 1400 to Oklahoma.

I think Sweet William knew better than we did that he had a job to do. To this day, I feel that, in his own way, he knew what it would take to do it. I know he was just as disappointed as I was when John Winnicki loaded him up and pulled away, leaving us all standing there ready to cry. I was sitting on a tree stump, and Joyce was standing by the corral feeding carrots to our newest recruit, Sea Ruler; Bea and Bob were looking on from the Winnebago.

All three horses were identical in color. March Along and Sweet William were identical in size and weight, and Sea Ruler was taller and leaner than the other two. Most people would look at these horse and say they were white, but horse people called them grey. Riding Sweet William only, we rode from Los Angeles to the Oklahoma border, by our route a distance of 1390 miles, in 75 days.

After sending Willie back to Tucson, I began riding both March and Ruler, alternating these horses as we rode toward the East Coast. This allowed me to ride every day with no days off for rest. We were previously resting Sweet William every five or six days. At that pace, we would finish in six months, which would be November. I wanted to finish in less than six months. With both horses, we were now averaging about 210 miles every seven days and some days rode 45 miles or more.

Now the question was: Could I keep up the pace? I was beginning to have problems with my knees and my back. In addition to our riding, I was exercising other muscles by running five miles each day to counterbalance the strain of riding. This helped, but my knees were beginning to feel the strain. I also had a hard time keeping my weight up, so I was now down to about 147 lbs. from a pre-ride weight of about 165. As a result, I had no rear end and was bruising my butt bones. This was very painful, and I often rode out of the saddle, standing in the stirrups or flexing my inner thigh to ride lighter in the saddle. I would often ask Brad if I was sitting properly and if he thought there were any adjustments I could make to relieve the pain. I could not understand how it could be so painful. There were no adjustments--I simply did not have enough butt muscle or fat for padding. After coming to this conclusion, I slowed my running to every other day so that I could put some weight back on. As a wrestler in high school, I remember dropping 20 lbs. every week to make weight at 126 lbs. The result: I was not able to sit for long periods of time in a hard chair.

Along the Oklahoma stretch, we did a lot of night riding. The horses and I liked the cool breezes and low traffic. It was tough on the support crew, though. We were bound and determined to ride every step of the way, and to do this, we had to get around many man-made obstacles when traffic was minimal. The night riding allowed us to do this.

At the end of each day's ride, we would note our stopping point with a marker, or circle the mile marker on the map. Finding those markers or that location in the dark the next morning was often a very frustrating experience. I can remember, on several occasions, we drove or walked for hours up and down a particular stretch of road looking for a marker.

We avoided riding at night on Friday and Saturday. In the United States, one out of three drivers on the road on a Friday or Saturday is impaired. A white horse and rider quickly appearing in the dark, as if from nowhere, on either the same side or on the oncoming side of the road is enough of a shock for a sober driver, let alone for someone who has had a few drinks. The odds were against us on Fridays and Saturdays, so we avoided those nights.

Bridges were an obstacle we had to contend with, plan for and scout in advance. On the interstate, the bridges have very little leeway, maybe five feet from the lane to the rail, sometimes less. Thus far on the ride, we had crossed dozens of these bridges, and our approach to this bridge on the North Fork of the Red River was fairly typical.

As we rode up to the bridge, it looked no different than the many interstate bridges we had crossed thus far. It was a little longer, and that always concerned me because it meant that trucks and cars were going by at high speeds within two or three feet of us for a longer period of time. Because we were riding with traffic, these vehicles would come up behind us very quickly and very close. There wasn't much room for error or for indecision. It was very hard to maneuver or to turn around if need be, so once we were on the bridge, our best bet was to keep moving forward. The sun was just coming up, and it was still a little dark out. We had become very accustomed to these interstate bridges. All of these factors, in combination with my preoccupation with the upcoming rest stop, caused me to ride into a very dangerous situation without thinking.

About one-half of the way across the bridge, we encountered a row of orange road markers in the leeway between the rail and the right lane. This automatically cut our five feet of clearance to about three feet, forcing us to skirt the markers and to ride closer to traffic. At this same point on the bridge, the middle two lanes were being repaired. All traffic on the bridge was being funneled through the far oncoming lane and the lane adjacent to us. Usually drivers would move over to the far lane when they saw us on a bridge, but in this case, they could not do that.

To add to the scene, the repair team started jack-hammering on the bridge, sending vibrations throughout the whole structure. Sea Ruler did not like this. Now, add one more variable to this muddle: a string of semi trucks, ten of them spaced 150 feet apart, going at least 80 miles per hour. These trucks were no more than 18 inches from us as we threaded the needle between the markers and the lane on this vibrating and pinging bridge. If I had stuck my left hand straight out, I would have been able to touch the trucks. Stopping would have made Sea Ruler even more nervous, so we kept walking.

It took the trucks about five minutes to get by. At that point, we were about two-thirds of the way across the bridge. Usually horses can handle frightening stimuli if they come in slowly and one at a time. In this case, they were coming from all directions at once, through Ruler's hooves in the form of vibrations, from the trucks 18 inches away, and from the unfamiliar orange markers that were teetering with the wind from the trucks. Had one of those markers fallen over and rolled around, Ruler might have immediately shied, possibly into our safety margin of 12 to 18 inches, and right into the lane. That would have been all she wrote.

We crossed the bridge without further incident. A very close call. In the future, I scouted all bridges and took nothing for granted. I began the trip in this cautious manner, taking nothing for granted and scouting everything. At this point we were just getting a little lazy and too comfortable. What we previously considered dangerous we now accepted as routine. That complacency was something that we had to avoid.

Later, when we started crossing more and more rivers, the construction of each bridge became of primary importance. Many bridges did not have concrete surfaces to ride across on, but were made of perforated steel so that water could drain through. This also allowed both me and the horse to see the river below. To add to the problem, these bridges also made a pinging noise when we were crossing on horseback and a roar or rumble as trucks and cars would pass. On some of the smaller bridges, there was a sidewalk with a rail. The problem with these bridges was that the rail was only slightly higher than the knee of the horse, and, if for some reason the horse shied toward this rail, it would be very easy at the dizzying height for him to panic and to bump up against the rail.

Our procedure in most cases, therefore, was to scout the bridge the day before and see if we could cross it without an escort. We observed the traffic patterns and asked about rush-hour time or whether traffic on the bridge was more congested on some days. We also asked about the construction of the bridge: Does it have a sidewalk or a berm that we can ride on? If we determined that I could do it without an escort, Brad would head on back to camp. If not, we would agree on a time and a place based on the conditions that day and the topography, and agree to meet just this side of the bridge at a given time.

I found out that late at night and early in the morning, before traffic, at about 4:30-5:00, were the best times to cross most bridges. Brad would meet us and lead us across the bridge. He would be traveling about 10 miles an hour, and I would trot with the horse's nose up against the back of the truck or the trailer, as close to the right side as possible. This I did for two reasons: so that Brad could see us in his right mirror out of the blind spot, and so that we were as far away as we could be from oncoming traffic. Vehicles coming up from behind would often be backed up for a mile when we were crossing some of the longer bridges. From the river below, it would have made an interesting picture to see a trailer with a horse and rider trotting right behind, and then immediately behind them a string of cars backed up for often a mile or more.

On another occasion, on this same stretch of interstate, I rode down through a small stream to avoid a bridge. This time I was riding March Along. After crossing the stream I found, much to my dismay, that we were now entangled in thick mesh netting used by the highway department to keep grass seed and foliage in place along the highway. March Along had EASY BOOTS on, and the clips on these boots got caught in the mesh.

If horses can't move their feet, they have a tendency to panic, especially on the side of a steep embankment. I didn't want March Along to get tangled in the mesh, panic, and roll down the hill. So I coaxed him up the hill, stopping every step to cut the netting off the clips. This unscheduled delay took about one hour, while Brad was patiently waiting at our water stop about a two-hour ride up the road.

Brad and Joyce are well known Arabian trainers and ranch managers, having been involved in the Arabian horse industry for over 35 years. Their renown was a big advantage to us as we hit the Midwest and later the East Coast. Bob and Bea were handling logistics, on-the-road media and fund-raising, as well as filming the ride. Bob, Bea, Brad and Joyce really got along well together. It was like a family of sorts; we had our good days and our bad days, but, regardless, we always got together at the end of the day for a happy hour.

Bea and Joyce would bring out appetizers before dinner, usually cheese and crackers and often, if we were taking the next day off, a beer or two, and we would sit around and talk about the events of that day or our activities the for next day. This was usually early in the evening, about 7:00 PM. I would be in bed within an hour or two. Brad and Bob and Bea and Joyce would stay up late talking and sharing stories. If we were taking the following day off, I'd stay up, too, and we would all sit around after dinner and talk about the area we were in and the people we met. Always the people. For example, Mr. Baskins, the blacksmith.

One day I saw Brad, off in the distance, standing next to the rig talking with somebody. This pick-up point was a typical point in the middle of nowhere, 150 miles in either direction to a city or town. As I rode up, Brad introduced me to Harry Baskins, a nationally known farrier (blacksmith). Baskins had seen Brad parked on the edge of the highway and had stopped to inquire if he needed any help. One thing led to another, and both Brad and I got a lesson on the iron anvil.

We learned that an iron anvil is not just a hunk of metal against which a blacksmith pounds horse shoes to shape them. It's a tool for the blacksmith, just as a paint brush is a tool for a painter. With an anvil, a blacksmith can shape a shoe to fit any horse. The design of the anvil, the type of material and the way the iron cures are very important. The ping or ring that an anvil makes when a blacksmith strikes it will tell you if you are working with a responsive or a dead anvil. Baskins told us that when you walk into a horse show, you can always tell by the ping of the anvil which blacksmith will be doing the most business. The best blacksmiths' anvils sing.

Baskins played a little song for us on his anvil, which was over 100 years old and was the original anvil that was patented at the turn of the century. Baskin's father was a blacksmith and designed the anvil and then passed the anvil, the patent, and the business on to his son. Baskins told us that every anvil that has been built since has been patterned after the Baskins anvil, but none have been able to capture the true design. Baskins gave both Brad and me a miniature of the larger anvil. They weigh about 6 ounces and are made of the same material and of the same design as the original. Baskins uses these miniature anvils as his calling cards. Brad told this story one evening at happy hour, and Bob and Bea wanted to get Baskins and his anvil on video.

Bea, Joyce, and I each kept a journal. We wrote every day. Sometimes we perceived incidents in the same manner, but often we saw events quite differently, as shown in our journals. Occasionally what I considered a significant episode on our journey, Bea or Joyce would not even mention in their journals, and vice versa.

For example, both Joyce and Bea wrote about our stay at Fort Cobb State Park near a small town called Albert, Oklahoma. I was numb at this point and made no reference in my journal to our stay at that park. We were riding now along Highway 152 toward Oklahoma City and passed through the town of Corn, a Mennonite community of about 1100 people. I was in the saddle, so the rest of the team stopped in

Corn to eat breakfast. Bea mentioned in her journal that they had Veronikas, a pancake rolled around dry cottage cheese mixed with egg and dipped in gravy. Joyce had steak and eggs. Bea went on to write later that day that we were camped now below the Fort Cobb State Park Dam. (This would not be the last time we camped below a dam.)

Bill and Kathy Orel owned the land and leased it to the state park, where employees had cleared a portion of it and have a vegetable garden, two port-o-johns, grills, a fireplace and picnic tables. They also had several horses in a field adjacent to this park. These new friends kept Ruler and March company. One of the horses was a pregnant mare, and she got so excited when she saw March and Ruler that she slipped and fell, rolling down the hill. Luckily, she was only three months pregnant and was not injured.

The Orels allowed us to use the facility at no charge as the State of Oklahoma's contribution to the rainforest. That evening, we went out for dinner at the Grubstake in Albert, which was owned by Bill Orels' cousin. The following encounter is out of Joyce's journal:

After dinner, I wanted to play some pool so we all crossed the street and walked into the only open bar I could find. It was a tavern with a juke box and three pool tables. It was ladies' night, $.25 draft beer. Our kind of place.

Brad and Joyce danced while Bea and Bob and I watched the pool tables in an attempt to determine who might easily be beaten. No sure bet anywhere--they were all really good. As Bob sized the place up, I tried to put quarters down on one table. There were too many quarters up, and they were all one man's quarters. This man had essentially tied the table up while he was winning, and then, if he lost, he had quarters down to keep on playing as well. The table was his. Noticing our frustration, the female bartender came over to talk with Bob. She explained the rules, which we already knew, but we thought of adding a new twist. We offered to buy the guy a beer so we could use the table. Brad and I started playing, and we were both on a roll, playing way over our heads and putting everything in. An impressive show, and one that attracted some attention.

Johnny, the player who held the table before us, came over and began talking with Bob. He told us, "Guys from Oklahoma don't have much else to do except work and play pool; that's why we're so good." This guy has his own cue. I should have known. Bob and Brad convinced Joyce and Bea to play Johnny for control of the table. Johnny could not believe he was going to play two women. About halfway through the game, the RIDE ACROSS AMERICA team got some lucky breaks and dropped 5 balls. Now they were even up with Johnny. Once, when it was Joyce's shot, Johnny went to the men's room, and Brad saw his chance--he dropped four of our balls in different pockets. Johnny came out and wouldn't believe Joyce shot them in. He accused us of cheating. The team started to get a bit nervous. Brad started to tease Johnny, gently at first, as only cowboys can. It worked and Johnny loosened up a bit, but made sure, by clearing the table, that the team knew that he was the best player in Albert. I saw nothing of this as I slept in the front seat of the car. The rest of the team came out of the tavern laughing, woke me up and on our ride back to camp told me what happened.

Bob and Bea were subtle pranksters. Brad told jokes and had a very large repertoire for any audience and Joyce was great with kids along the way. She was also our people person--she talked with everybody that would stop and visit the camp for as long as they wanted to talk.

Bea was deathly afraid, it seemed to me, of bugs and spiders. Joyce, too, would often comment on the buggy conditions. I saw all this as an opportunity to frighten Bea. One day late in my ride, I saw a snake on the side of the road. Further inspection showed it to be only a snake skin, a perfect prop for a prank I wanted to play on Bea. Snake skin has a very peculiar feel to it and, just by looking at it, you know how it would feel to touch it. I was not a stranger to the sensation. As a youngster, I had snakes for pets and had a real sense of what they felt like. Upon my return to camp, I made a point of visiting the Winnebago and quietly dropped the snakeskin right next to the Kachina dolls.

Several days went by, and I questioned Brad and Joyce to see if they had seen any particular reaction. No reaction thus far. After two days, there was still no reaction. We had no days off now so I was usually dead beat when I hit the sack. It never took more than a minute to fall asleep, but this one evening was to be a little different than most.

Sound asleep after about two hours, I was tossing and turning to get comfortable, and my leg rubbed up against something very rough and dense. I immediately woke up. I had a snake in my bed. It was definite. The snake wasn't moving. I told myself: Calmly, wake up slowly, think before you react, don't make any quick moves. As I began to become more conscious, I attempted to formalize a plan to debilitate this snake. A bright light might confuse the snake long enough for me to roll off the bed. Chanting "One, two, three," I flicked on the lights, threw off the covers and rolled out of the bed.

There lay the snakeskin. I was not going to give my team members the satisfaction of knowing how shocked I was to wake up in bed with a snake. This snakeskin passed back and forth between all three vehicles in this manner for the next month. No one said a word to anyone or expressed shock to find it in the blender, in the bed, under the pillow . . . in shoes. I think Bob and Bea ended up with the skin and drove all the way to Connecticut before they found it.

Riding on toward Oklahoma City, we passed a town called Nowhere, Oklahoma. Now, I must tell you about Nowhere. It is the hardest place to find, bar none. You never actually arrive in Nowhere because, once you get there, you are not in Nowhere but instead you are NOW HERE. Frustrating.

We rode through Oklahoma City in a deluge of rain--seven straight days of rain. The ground was so soft that March Along stretched a tendon and came up lame. Brad had him rest for 15 days, and I rode Sea Ruler for the next two weeks straight, still averaging over 21 miles per day and often 26 and 27 miles. I think March Along pulled a tendon in the deep mud. All that mud sucking at his hooves for 25 miles probably pulled and twisted the horse's feet in every direction at once.

We were now beginning to encounter many rivers and streams. I crossed the Canadian River in Oklahoma in the early morning, beginning that ride at midnight. We crossed the Arkansas River in the early morning as well.

This stretch was tough. Mixed in with all of the pranks and good times were some very emotional events--the switch in Cordell with Ruler and Willy, the increase in pace, the cancellation of two key fund-raisers and the consequent tension. The overall conditions were still upbeat, but we had now been on the road for several months with no rest, no R & R. We could not afford any time off, and my insistence to maintain the pace was unnerving. I call it the emotional roller coaster affect.

Oklahoma was a stretch of extremes--giant swings in mood from total elation, pranks and good times, to total depression, the switch with Willy and the ongoing and up tempo pace, the routine and rhythm, on and on.

6

WE HIT THE WALL INSIDE OURSELVES

Missouri and Illinois

If Oklahoma was the calm before the storm, I think we started our sprint to the finish about 500 miles too soon. Our elation was premature. Soon thereafter, somewhere between Tulsa, Oklahoma, and Joplin, Missouri, I hit the wall. The wall is the point in a race when you ask yourself, "What in the h--- am I doing out here?"

It was hot, 100 degrees, and so humid you could cut the air with a knife. This combination--wet heat and fatigue, mosquitoes, ticks, flies and gnats--began to do a real tap dance on my head. We were all getting more than a little road-weary. I was taking pain killers for breakfast along with my normal can of pineapple and cereal. This helped kill the pain in my knees and my butt bones. I was now seventeen pounds lighter than at the start.

We had all been on the road now for more than three months. The close quarters and long hours were beginning to show on the whole team, with the exception of the horses. The horses were getting stronger and we were now averaging a little over 25 miles per day. But the honeymoon was over. The adrenaline we produced at the start was gone, and we had just begun to realize how far we still had to go.

On August 23, 1989, we crossed into Missouri at a point just east of Joplin. This point is the center of a four-state region that includes Oklahoma, Missouri, Arkansas, and Kansas. As I was crossing the border into Missouri out of Oklahoma, the Joplin newspaper caught us. The pictures taken by the reporters reveal that point in the journey was truly the wall. We were hurting in every sense of the word. If, at that point, the rest of the team was doing as badly as I looked, I can understand our morale problem.

Two funny things happened in Joplin. The first was a fluke. I was, at this point, a little tired of repeating to people along the way the same old story about my ride and the rainforest. The response was always so strange when I told them I was riding to New York from Los Angeles. They would often want to talk, and that time really added up. We couldn't afford the delay. The farther east we rode the harder it was to complete a day's ride. Everyone wanted to stop and talk. Although we knew that we had to talk about the rainforest at every opportunity, by this time it was becoming very tiring. So toward the end of some days I would catch myself saying to people who would ask where I was going: "I am simply riding to the next town. By the way, how far is that?" Or sometimes I would almost automatically hand them a brochure and a brief explanation, and keep on riding. This usually worked, but one time I got caught.

We arrived in Joplin the day before a big article came out in the paper and on the news. I wanted to purchase some clothes and needed to get some pants altered at the Polo store in Joplin. I had lost so much weight that my pants no longer fit, and I needed them for the fund-raiser in St. Louis. At the store, the clerk said," Fine. Come back in two days and we'll have them ready for you." As we were making small talk, the clerk asked if I was in town on business or pleasure. I responded," Neither." He looked at me as if to say "What else is there?" I did not give any further explanation. I was very tired and still sweaty from the ride that day. Having had a wake-up that morning at 4:30 AM and one scheduled the next day for 4:00 AM, I was only looking forward to a shower and a nap.

The clerk kept looking at me as if he needed a better answer. So I said, "I was just passing through town and would only be there for a few days: I'm heading east." This seemed to satisfy him. I left.

Little did I know that the coverage the next day would be extensive with articles on both TV stations, the radio and both papers, front page. Bob Shepard had outdone himself in Joplin--he had the media buzzing about the event.

My return to the store two days later was comical. The clerk alerted the rest of the staff, and they all came out, chanting in unison, "Just heading east, eh? Real slow, we might add," and, laughing hysterically, they all went back to their jobs. The clerk asked me why I didn't tell him what I was doing in town. I responded that I was simply too tired to go through another explanation that day. He replied, "After seeing your interview on the TV the evening before, I can understand that. You did and still do look beat." I said, "Thanks for the encouragement."

The interview on TV with KOAM in Joplin was interesting. Kevin Petrehn, KOAM's premiere reporter, wanted to do a really unique interview. So he got a horse and rode along beside me. Kevin had, however, never been on a horse before and was carrying camera equipment and microphones. The video of that interview, filmed by Bob Shepard, showed Kevin shooting footage and interviewing me as he was riding half on and half off his horse. I was on his left and he was leaning well to his right and the camera equipment was dangling everywhere. His horse was walking sideways in an attempt to stay under Kevin. A good horse will do that, and we got a perfect example on film.

The TV spot came out fine, and we gave Kevin rainforest footage as well. Kevin and KOAM did a great job on the spot. It was the best yet, well worth the time and effort we all spent setting it up. CNN used this cut several weeks later on an Earth Matters segment featuring our ride together with a guy who flew an ultralight across Greenland for another environmental cause.

On August 26th we went up to St. Louis for two fund-raisers. We broke camp that morning and Brad put me on Sea Ruler at 4:30 AM. I rode 26 miles that day, got off Ruler about 2:30 PM and then drove about 450 miles to St. Louis. We took the following day off to attend both events. We then drove back to our stopping point in southern Missouri to continue our ride. Jim Volz had an evening fund-raiser for us, and earlier that same afternoon we brought Sea Ruler down to the arch in downtown St. Louis for a photo shoot and rainforest rally. We left March Along with a friend of Brad's at our stopping point in southern Missouri. This gave March Along a much needed day of rest so he was ready to go the day after our fund-raiser. Sea Ruler was a little tired from the trailer ride to St. Louis.

Both events went very well and we had more than 150 people attend the fund-raiser at Jim Volz's farm. I got a picture of Brad carrying a SAVE THE RAINFOREST picket sign under the arch in St. Louis. I never thought I would see the day that Brad would carry a picket sign in downtown St. Louis. All we needed to do now was to get him to wear a SAVE THE RAINFOREST T-SHIRT. Never.

These fund-raisers were good because they broke up the routine, but they were also very tough on the team and the horses. While we were on the road and riding, we were in a rhythm of sorts. Our routine was very important--it kept us going. The activities, however, were very tiring because we always had to look our best and act as if we were not weary and look as though we were having fun. Given the pace we were trying to maintain daily, that facade was very difficult to sustain.

If a child asked us, "Are you having fun?," even if we weren't, I always said," Yes" and smiled and shook hands with everybody. All I really wanted to do was crawl into a nice bed and sleep for more than five hours. I knew that the next day these people would all go home and sit comfortably reading about us in the paper, while we would be up at 3:00 AM riding through some rainstorm in the dark for three hours, and then in the heat of the day for seven more hours. The fund-raisers were as draining as the riding because I did not slack off. We did not rest before or after the events. We immediately got back on the road.

The strain of riding affected us in other ways. What were previously little differences of opinion in our group now started to gain in size and frequency. I wrote in my journal on August 28th that I almost "lost it." Differences were building between Brad and me.

I was pushing very hard and would often ask Brad to double up with two horses and put in 45 miles on back-to-back days. This was as tough on me and the team members as it was on the horses. From Texas on we rode very hard with many 10-and 12-hour days--non-stop. I was bitterly opposed to days off and made it very clear that we would ride every day. And this included inclement weather and storms. We would make every effort to work around vehicle problems so we could continue riding.

August 28th, 4:30 AM: The rain was coming down in sheets and the wind was buffeting the trailer in waves that made it rattle and shake. I was sitting at the table in the dark, eating out of a can of pineapple and crunching on granola cereal. I had cans and buckets strategically placed around the trailer to catch the water that was dripping in from the leaks in the roof. Everything in my trailer was leaking and everything in it was soaked--clothes, bed, food. March had just pulled up a bit gimpy going through Oklahoma City. So Ruler was carrying the load, and I was still pushing for the mileage.

Brad was concerned: There were flash flood warnings and the rain was coming down in waves. Sometimes we could not see 20 feet in front of us. I was wearing a yellow rain suit which Joyce had bought for Brad and me at a K-Mart, and they were no different from the ones I had worn as a young child; I even had the little yellow rain hat. I looked like an older version of Donald Duck. We had been riding in this weather for four days with one good horse.

I had spoken often by phone with my business partners, Luis Lugo and Joe Tooker, in Tucson and the news was not good. I played a key role in those businesses and, when I left, some important work was not getting done. I felt very guilty about that and tried to help while I was on the road, but to no avail. We were losing the business and there wasn't a damn thing I could do about it. To keep riding was a very difficult sacrifice to make because it affected others: we had employees and I had partners who depended on me. Neither my partners nor I felt at the time that the marketing and contracting end of the business would deteriorate as quickly as it did. We also got caught in an economic downturn of sorts which just added to our dilemma.

On August 28th, 4:30 AM, Brad vetoed my decision to ride that day. I was livid. I felt his decision was motivated less by the poor riding conditions and more by personal comfort. So I let him know how I felt.

I told Brad I thought that we should ride and that the weather should not be a factor. We had been riding in the rain very uncomfort-ably now for four days, and I was prepared to continue riding in it. Brad replied that we were risking injury. I retorted that it was no more risky now than on any other day of the week.

I never tried to overrule Brad, but I had oftened questioned his reasoning. I did not do this in a disrespectful way, but in an inquisitive manner. His logic often escaped me, and I wanted to know why it was this way or why it was that way.

I found out later that it was very hard for Brad to show or tell me why he decided to do this or that because often it was a "seat of the pants" or "gut feel" reasoning on his part. With horses, only experience explains that. And that is something that is difficult to explain to anyone. When it came to the horse-related issues, even though I disagreed, Brad still had the final say. Sometimes though there was a grey area of decision-making that involved the horse, the vehicles, the weather, the other people on the ride, the roads we were traveling and our commitment to stay on schedule. In that grey area I had the final say, but, like the President, Brad could veto the whole day by canceling the ride on a horse-related issue. This did not happen often and we were usually able to come to some kind of consensus or agreement, but at a price.

The price was that, in this grey area of decision-making, our tension had begun to build. We often had disagreements over the route I chose to ride. My concern was time; comfort and convenience were a secondary concern. So I often chose the straightest, shortest route and this route was often very uncomfortable for the other members of the team and very inconvenient to trailer into and out of. It did, however, save time. I also wanted to ride every day and go as far as we could. In some cases, it was more than Brad felt the horses should go.

We were not arguing--we never raised our voices at each other--but, instead, the comraderie was substantially reduced. At the end of the day we would go our separate ways and not speak until the next morning.

I am, for the most part, a quietly driven and persistent person and I demand a lot of myself and from the people around me. I have a very high energy level and I try to lead by example and don't often verbalize what I am thinking. This can be a problem, because the more focused I become, the more quiet I get and I often assume that those around me are as committed as I to whatever project we are working on at the time. Brad and Joyce and Bob and Bea were all certainly as committed as I. But Brad, in his own way, tempered my drive, both consciously and subconsciously, with a sense of moderation. When I focus in on something, I prioritize everything and all the nonessentials go out of the window. On the ride, I did this often with eating and sleeping. Consequently, Joyce and Bea were constantly trying to force me to eat.

After our confrontation, Bob called us to the trailer and we all sat down and talked it out. I didn't hold anything back, nor did Brad. This kind of tense confrontation was understandable considering the strenuous circumstances, close quarters and road fatigue. This was no leisurely stroll across America. We were not only trying to break a record, but also to establish a new unbeatable record. I knew I had only one shot at doing this and I wanted us to set a well-documented record that would stand the test of time. I knew that as soon as we set the record and it became public, numerous individuals would be out to break it. I know, because in 1982 I organized a group of scuba divers to set a Guinness Book World Record.

We rode a bicycle underwater 64.96 miles in 62 hours. We held that record for the longest underwater bicycle race for less than one year. As soon as the Guinness Book came out with our record in it, the record became public and was quickly broken by first, a group going 100 miles in that same time-frame, and then a second group who went 120 miles. I did not want this to happen to our Ride Across America, so my thoughts were that a one-rider and a three-horse ride from coast to coast in five months or less would be unbreakable.

In retrospect, Brad's sense of moderation was a very important component and essential to our success, not just because it pertained to the horses but also to me and other members of the team. With a moderating force to rely upon, I pushed hard assuming that he would do his part and say, "Back off," or "Slow down." If I didn't have that back-up or balance from Brad I would have done it myself. I was, in a subconscious way, relying on Brad to set my pace. Even though I resented it when he said it, I knew it was important, and this push and pull kept us going.

During the ride, a lot of the aggravation had to do with the fact that we were together so much. It was simply a case of two people, very different in many ways and very much the same in other ways, getting to know each other intimately under extreme physically demanding circumstances.

On that same day I wrote in my journal that I needed to stay in touch with all my old friends, and I even listed them all. I made a commitment to work harder at my business. I wrote: "that I wanted to finish the ride as a thank you for the many people who helped us: "I feel a growing burden to finish and that burden comes from all of the well wishers along the way. We are now riding as much for them as we are for the issue and ourselves."

I ended the journal that day with three comments: The first is something Bazy Tankersley, the owner of Al-Marah Arabians, told me before we left. She said, "in this kind of event, to finish is to win."

Immediately after that, I wrote: "Nothing of any real significance was ever accomplished that did not require extreme sacrifice."

Finally I wrote: "If number one and number two are true, then keep it together, whatever it takes."

On that day it seems I was little nostalgic, a little lonesome for home, and more than a little tired. At that point I was on automatic and not all that coherent. I cannot remember details from that part of the ride. The start and the finish are vivid, while the middle 1000 miles are vague. One long 45-day blur. It was almost as if I were sleep-riding.

On September 1st, things began to take a turn for the better. We had some really good press coverage in Joplin and just after that I was riding up into a little town called Grambia. We were now riding in Missouri, adjacent to Arkansas. At various points along the way I had been calling in to WJR radio in Detroit to report on our progress and to answer questions about the rainforest, live on the air. Francesca did a good job of setting this up for us. You must understand that this was very difficult to coordinate. We were typically riding through very unpopulated areas and finding a phone at the exact time I needed to be on the air was next to impossible.

Gas stations, private homes, car phones, a police station, city hall-- you name it, and we used it. My attempt to find a phone while riding a horse down the road would have been a perfect advertisement for MCI. You can imagine some of the conversations I would get into trying to convince a local farmer to let me use his private rotary phone to make a long distance call to Detroit while holding my white Arabian horse and talking about the rainforest issue. I can remember some very comical situations. I think some of these people may have been on the verge of calling in the local law enforcement agency. If it weren't for the brochures I carried in my saddle, I probably would have been incarcerated.

I asked WJR why I couldn't make these calls later in the day after I got off the horse. The problem was that this particular show aired in the morning at 10:00 AM. Keep in mind, we were riding west to east and the time difference was one, two or three hours, depending on our location.

I would complete the day's ride at between noon and 2:00 PM. That would mean that I would need to make my phone calls at 7:00, 8:00, 9:00, 10:00 or possibly 11:00 AM depending on how close we were and if we were west or east of Detroit. Ordinarily, this would not seem like a difficult task to coordinate, but I was looking for a phone on a road I didn't know, trying to convince strangers to let me use their phones. Added to that, I was riding a white horse, dressed more like a runner than a rider, and carrying an MCI calling card. I lucked out on September 3rd: I had a telephone call set up for 9:15 AM Missouri time with WJR. The arrangement was that I had to be on the air and on hold by 10:10 AM their time (9:10 AM my time) or they would cancel until the next day.

At 8:55 AM I was still two miles outside of the little town of Grambia. I wasn't wearing a watch, but asked a passerby what time it was. So that left me 20 minutes to canter in the last two miles. I began riding at a very fast trot through the small community, asking people right and left: "Where is the closest phone?" They all pointed down the road, saying, "Quick Stop."

I arrived in the center of town at the Quick Stop at 9:09 AM. So I now had one minute to find someone to hold my horse Sea Ruler, get inside the Quick Stop and make the call from the payphone just inside the door. People inside the Quick Stop watched with strange looks on their faces, as I walked up to the door and held it open, still hanging onto Ruler. With one hand I reached for the phone, while Ruler proceeded to stand on the sidewalk blocking the door so no one could leave the store. Luckily, I got through to the program coordinator, Rosanna Kelly, but was immediately put on hold to wait for five minutes until the show began.

No one in the store said a word, but they were still staring. Ruler was now nudging me. He had moved so that he was standing inside the doorframe in the store. I now had five minutes to organize this little fiasco so I could finish the pending talk show. I already had everyone's attention so, seeing no other alternative, I broke the silence by announcing to everyone: "I am on the air in Detroit on a long distance call for a talk show. Would someone please hold my horse?" No reaction.

Ruler now had half his front end in the store and was gumming the potato chip rack. I mentioned that I was riding across America on this horse. Luckily, someone inside the store recognized us, and immediately everyone broke into smiles. Three customers offered to hold Ruler while I completed my phone call. The owner offered me a bottle of juice and a sandwich "on the house" and then called the local paper to do an interview as well. The coverage we had received the day before and that morning in Joplin helped them all make the connection. After the talk show interview, I stayed for a while to talk to the local media and several of the people and then rode on down the road.

That same day I found out that we were only about 60 miles from Fayetteville, Arkansas, a town I had lived in many years ago. That brought back a lot of memories. I wrote in my journal: "Twenty-seven years ago I lived in this area and it seems like such a long time ago. If I had known at that time that I would be riding a horse through here 27 years hence to save the rainforest, would that have made any significant difference?" I added: "In this day and time you predict the future based on present day criteria, no longer on past history. History is no longer a good indicator of what the future will be." Changes are constant and exponential. What previously might have been a sound process for making a personal or financial decision will not be so under present and future circumstances. Those who recognize this and are able to adapt and are willing to be flexible will succeed.

A perfect example, I wrote, was the S&L crisis and the Third World debt. Who would have thought in 1975 that lending money to a country would be a bad idea? Countries don't go broke, people do, we always thought. Who would have guessed that loans based on oil projections both in Texas as well as in Third World countries would be a bad bet? S&L's, as they diversified, lent money against oil assets across the country and lost everything.

I also wrote that we did not know years ago that, within 50 years, some aspects of technology would have a devastating impact on our environment. That history is no longer a predictor of the future, and that as yet undeveloped new technology will have the greatest single impact on our lives and this environment, has struck a chord of concern in us. Our future is now officially uncertain. That is scary.

The implications, both positive and negative, for societies as we think of them today are limitless. It is both scary and exciting. (While riding on a horse on such a long journey I had a lot of time to think.) I wrote that same day: "Maybe I should think less. This is too deep to fathom. I need to leave all this up to politicians, scientists and philosophers." And then I added, "What a combination! If we do that we are in deep trouble."

On September 1st we pulled into Montauk Park in southern Missouri. A state park located at the headwaters of the Current River, Montauk serves as a fish hatchery and fishing park. We camped here for five days.

Montauk is probably one of the most beautiful fishing spots in the United States. As we were driving down into the park, it seemed so very familiar, and I quickly recalled that, when I was six or seven years old, my family came here from Arkansas in the summer. The place had not changed in those 26 years at all. I found the rural road system in Missouri was also unchanged and just as frustrating in 1989 as it had been in 1963 when our family drove through this area. In our ride we tried in all cases to stay as close to a straight-line route as we possibly could. This forced us to pore over maps in the Midwest and quiz local farmers on the shortest or straightest possible route from point A to point B.

In the northern Ozarks of southern Missouri, the straightest and shortest path is often two very different routes. The terrain and the riding conditions along the road are of utmost concern in this area. Often in Missouri we were on one-and two-lane rural roads and local trails. The rural roads were marked with a letter designation. For example, the roads around Montauk Park were marked as LL, LM, LK and JJ. Roads farther east and south were marked with other letter combinations.

Once Brad and I were talking with a local store owner about our route. We needed to get to a point about 45 miles farther east along as straight a route as possible. According to the notes in my journal, the directions went something like this: "Take LL about two miles and get off on 168; it's a fire trail. That will take you to F; at F go east about 6 miles and get on CC or AA, either one will take you to PP. There are several roads that run parallel and perpendicular to AA and CC. Don't take them, they include U, WW, H and JJ, they are all dead ends. Stay on CC or AA until you get to B; when you hit B take it east past M and P to Z; Z east will put you within spitting distance of the Mississippi river. Good Luck."

No kidding! Somewhere in there is a mistake. See if you can find it--we did. It took us three days to cover 45 miles. Nonetheless, that still saved us about four days, since the more northerly route would have taken seven days.

We made it to the river, and on September 9th we crossed the Mississippi at a city called Chester. We were now in Illinois. I was riding March Along and had left Sea Ruler back at camp to rest for about two days. Two days earlier, on September 7th, we had a freak accident that almost ended the trip. We were riding along PP, a narrow rural road with a very steep drop on both sides; we were straddling the top of the road and the embankment. A small hill was in the distance, and coming up behind us was a tractor with a hay wagon hooked on behind. The tractor was in the center of the road. Just as we approached the hill, the tractor pulled up next to us, and, as we began to crest it together, the tractor swerved closer to us to make room for any oncoming traffic that could be on the other side. This pushed Ruler and me right off the edge of the road and we began walking awkwardly sideways about 25 percent of the way down the embankment.

At this point Ruler stepped into a huge hole, at least six feet deep, and went down. I rolled out of the saddle to my right and down the hill in an attempt to take whatever pressure I could off Ruler. As I started to roll down the hill, I caught myself and looked to my left just in time to see Ruler rolling down the hill right behind me. He was out of control, as this was a very steep embankment. He rolled right over me and crunched me. I continued rolling and sliding down to the bottom of the embankment. Then Ruler was up and shaking himself off. The saddle was hanging underneath him and he had grass stains and dirt all over him. I walked him slowly along a fenceline at the bottom of the embankment and then back up to the road. He limped for about a mile, and then, miraculously, he shook it off. Sometimes the best way to keep a injury down is to walk it off. In this case it worked and we kept on going.

Now the team was being extraordinarily careful. The farther we rode, the more meticulous I became, and our planning each evening in some cases took several hours. I wanted to confirm every detail. This sometimes meant while I was riding, Brad spent the greater part of his day driving alternate routes in an attempt to determine the straightest, shortest, and safest possible path. Planning inevitably involved a trade-off between three variables: (1) danger, narrow rural roads and embankments versus interstate and traffic, (2) time and distance, (3) people comfort. Often the straightest route was the most dangerous and least comfortable for the support team. We needed to consider all of these factors as the ride was as much a people event as it was a horse event. Some days we spent as much time scouting and talking to local residents as we did riding. Some scouting trips brought us in as late as midnight; then we needed to prepare for a 4:00 or 5:00 AM wake-up call. It was raining every day now and Joyce wrote in her journal: "It is amazing how we go from L.A. to Texas without a drop of rain and then we are hit daily." Riding in the rain was miserable. The horses hated it, I hated it and it is hard on morale. On September 11th, despite the rain, I covered 38.4 miles using both horses. We were going to try this extra distance every fourth day. Joyce wrote in her journal, "At this pace we will be in D.C. in no time flat." She mentioned the date, October 15th.

On September 13, we crossed into Indiana. I was nodding off as we rode down a lonely rural road and missed a turn that I needed to take toward the Wabash River and the Indiana border. Brad had left us about an hour's ride from the bridge and was going to meet us there as we crossed into Indiana. He arrived and we were nowhere to be found. As Brad backtracked looking for us, he found where Highway 14 and Highway 1 meet and then, several miles later, split off, Highway 1 going north on the Illinois side and Highway 14 heading east across the Wabash. Brad asked a man at the intersection if he'd seen a man riding a grey horse. The man pointed north up highway 1.

Brad found Ruler and me trotting along, going the wrong way. He drove up and said matter-of-factly, "How is the ride going today?"

"Fine," I said,"Only thing is, I thought I should have crossed the Wabash by now, maybe it's up around the next corner."

"Yeah maybe, if you're riding around the world, because that is the only way you are going to reach the Wabash by riding in this direction," Brad said.

I said "Oh, no. Wrong way." This was the first time in 2000-plus miles we had gone the wrong way. I turned around and finally crossed into Indiana late in the day on September 13th. My little detour north up Highway 1 cost us about two hours riding time.

Riding at night up to, through, and away from many large cities and small towns, I was impressed with the glow that I could see from many miles away. The city would twinkle and I would always wonder why. I'm told that, as electricity feeds a community, it surges through the power lines and the twinkle you see from far away is a result of that surge. It prompted me to think: "What great amounts of energy we use in America." All that light is energy which comes from the earth as coal and is produced in coal-burning power plants.

In the United States we also use energy from other sources-- nuclear, solar, natural gas, wind--just to name a few. But primarily we burn coal to generate electricity. In southern Illinois and parts of Missouri we mine high-sulfur coal to use in these generators. As we burn high-sulfur coal and coal in general, we spew ash and particulates as well as sulfur dioxide into the air. Sulfur dioxide together with nitrogen oxide from car exhausts are two of the chief contaminants in acid rain.

Nitrogen oxide can come from these same coal-burning generators, but mostly it comes from the growing number of automobiles. I thought: "How comfortable we all are in our electric homes, with air-conditioning in our cars and offices."

While I was riding, I could have been living in the nineteenth century. On the remote roads and trails we rode we were living a very low-energy existence. One horse power per mile. I don't know if they even make motors that small. The lonesome riding caused me to reflect: "What if I really had to get from place to place by horse? Could society get along without petroleum, natural gas and coal? Doubtful. We know our fossil fuel supplies are finite and that we will eventually run out of these fuels some day. Can we replace them? Undoubtly yes, we will--with new technology. But when? When it becomes cost-effective to do so or when our present sources of energy become too expensive. What will these alternatives be? In the interim period, as we discover new alternatives and as we use up our present sources, what do we do?

We will run out. It may not be in our lifetime, or that of our children, but soon thereafter we will run out. As I look back I see very clearly that Americans and people in general respond as consumers to an impact personally only if it involves their own money. When it hurts us financially, we change. The most recent and significant example I can think of is the OPEC oil embargo in the mid 1970's. The result: higher prices at the gas pump. Our reaction and that of people worldwide was immediate: Reduce our dependence on oil. This we did very quickly. Why?

Because it hurt us in the pocketbook. We began passing legislation that required more fuel-efficient automobiles and we began searching frantically for alternatives. I saw this transition take place, and then I saw it swing back the other way. The Middle East is a very volatile region, with Iraq's recent invasion of Kuwait oil prices have begun to fluctuate dramatically once again. Our immediate move to defend our oil interests in this region simply underscores once again that an oil based economy is a house of cards both economically and environmentally.

OPEC no longer controls the oil market and the oligopoly it once had is gone. The result is that the price of a barrel of oil dropped significantly over the next 17 years. Interestingly enough, the price of oil at the pump did not. Which meant that in between the barrel and the pump someone was taking a big piece of the action, or it meant that the delivery of oil to the consumer had become much more expensive. I speculate it was a little of both, with a lean toward the profit-taking side.

Nevertheless, we were able to change. We did in this particular situation respond to the oil crisis by cutting back. Over the next 17 years, however, we became accustom to the higher gas prices at the pump and we now use more gas than we previously did. So we know we can cut back, but we don't. Why?

We have a crisis on our hands now that is of much greater significance. It is two-fold.

First, we are once again growing more dependent on oil, gas, and fossil fuels in general. World consumption is increasing and as we consume more, we jeopardize future generations' access to these same resources.

Most importantly, we are damaging the planet by consuming these products. We have the technology to produce fuel-efficient automobiles, but we don't. Why? Consumers do not demand that we produce fuel-efficient vehicles.

One alternative that has a lot of promise is solar energy. Solar energy has been around for a long time. Once it is in place, it is far and above the most environmentally sound and least expensive systems to operate. It is also passive and relatively maintenance free. Why do we not move to this alternative right now?

Cost. Typically the average homeowner can install a gas system for $1500 while a comparable solar system will cost several thousand dollars. In other parts of the world, solar energy has an excellent track record and its success worldwide should warrant further research and investment.

Within the earth is heat that can be brought to the surface in the form of steam or hot water. This can then be converted to produce electricity, providing us with another source of energy--geothermal energy. Many countries, including the United States, are tapping geothermal power. Japan and Iceland are leaders in the technology and many say that it could, sometime in the 20th century, develop into a significant market. Once again, exploration, experimentation, and research are expensive. Discovering its full potential is simply a matter of "when," when other sources become more expensive.

Hydroelectric power has been universally accepted worldwide. It is a relatively safe energy source and, in it's operational mode, is more or less compatible with the environment. It does do extensive damage to local habitat and in some areas, for example in the Brazilian rainforest, these projects have destroyed ecologically important habitat, caused flooding and wiping out indigenous populations. There are some dramatic and as yet undefined environmental impacts that are just now surfacing. The change in water temperature and the potential catastrophic impact from a dam failure are a cause of concern to environmentalists and governments. The cost in some cases is prohibitive. Furthermore, the technology is still somewhat limited.

In the future these and other alternatives will begin to play a bigger and bigger role in meeting our overall energy needs. The 1970's proved that energy conservation was effective. It is apparent, however, that the typical consumer will not, of his own accord, take aggressive steps to conserve energy. We take energy for granted and will only respond to a crisis in the marketplace. Today the market does not truly reflect the cost of energy consumption. We need the government to step in and provide encouragement and incentive. Experimentation and research for alternatives must continue and this will only happen if the price is right. Right now, it is not. Until we can develop more appropriate alternatives, energy conservation on the part of the consumer and government intervention to promote further research and incentives are required.

The very important relationship that we must understand is that we consumers place a demand on the market that the market will attempt to meet. In most cases we place a demand for ecologically inappropriate products. Our demand is the driving force behind what we consume and produce. We must very quickly become aware of that relationship and learn to harness that potential.

We as consumers, must demand that producers provide alternative products. What people in this country want (and feel entitled to) is having their cake and eating it at the same time. This is and will continue to be the underlying frustration of the ecology movement. The problems in America are linked to issues of too much, rather than too little. The ecology movement must become more linked to economic problems and less to ideology. I believe that ecological ideology in general has ignored the context of economic development from which the problems of pollution have been generated. We must bring the two closer together.

Where our energy comes from

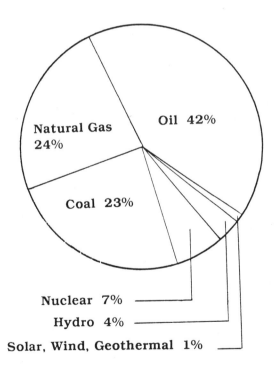

All decimals have been rounded
to the nearest whole number.

Courtesy of United States Department of Energy

7

THE ENVIRONMENTAL PARADIGM

Indiana, Kentucky and Ohio

By September 14th, we were in Indiana. It was raining--had been for about five days straight. I've included a picture one reporter took of Sea Ruler and me on that day. She stopped to talk with us about the ride, after she found us soaked to the bone, riding along a rural road in southern Indiana. It was raining so hard she would not get out of the car, but she did say she was excited to meet us and drove 300 miles that day to find us. It was a miserable interview, but the resulting article was very good.

Later that day I sat in my trailer, feeling miserable. It was still raining and I had just completed the day's ride--23.7 miles. My trailer was custom built specifically to transport and house both people and horses for a short period of time, at a horse show, for example. It was built in the late 1970s, and, before Al-Marah bought it specifically for this ride, it was sitting idle in the back of a ranch in Arizona. To say it needed some work was an understatement.

The living area was 10 feet by 20 feet and included a bathroom, kitchen, table and couch. The sleeping area was a shelf which jutted out of one side of the main cabin, with steps leading up to it. It was the same width as the cabin but only 15 feet long. The major discomfort of the sleeping area was the height: it was only 4 feet. So I had to crawl up into the sleeping cabin in the evening and crawl out and dress down below in the morning. This was a real inconvenience when Sheryl and I were both sharing the trailer for the first 600 miles.

The trailer leaked, and the stove, air conditioner, and heater did not work. We did not discover the air-conditioning malfunction until we were in Oklahoma, so it was hot in that trailer. As the heater also did not work, I would when necessary heat the place each night by turning on all of the gas burners for about 20 minutes. However, since I did not start doing this until we hit the east coast, I only ran the risk of

It's raining in Indiana. Sea Ruler and Lucian stop for a interview in Selvin, Indiana.
Courtesy of Betsy Stanton

79

blowing up the whole trailer for a period of about 20 days. That is probably why I slept so well at night those last 20 days--gas--and why I was so groggy at wake-up time each morning at 4:00 AM. I think we had a small leak in the propane line.

Now the most difficult and disagreeable problem: The back of this trailer was a two-horse stall. I lived in the front, and the horses rode in the back. Although they did not sleep in the back--they slept outside in a pen--boy, was it smelly in the trailer! I was the only one on the team who could tolerate eating or even simply sitting in there. I had become accustomed to the smell. Most of the clothes I had on the ride still smell like horse manure. It was really bad in the West and Midwest with the heat, and only got worse with the humidity and rain as we traveled east. Also, the smell attracted bugs into the trailer. To me, it wasn't all that bad, but then I had no alternative. Obviously, we were not able to do any interviews in my trailer.

This trailer, with all of its shortcomings, acted as our transport to and from our base camp and our starting and stopping point each day. This meant that every morning I had to uproot and unhook my home, tie everything down, and load the horse or horses for that day's ride. Then we had to attach the trailer to the pick-up truck and head out to our stopping point from the previous day's ride to begin again that morning. But eventually we got this down to a science and could do all of this in less than 10 minutes.

Living conditions in Brad's and Joyce's trailer were considerably nicer. They had all of the conveniences of home, but in a much smaller version, still a little cramped for a five-month trip, but not all that bad. Bob and Bea, however, were a completely different story. They were traveling in high style. The Winnebago they had was a house on wheels. Full living room, kitchen, dining and sleeping area. Bob had all kinds of video equipment, a veritable studio with a satellite dish on top and three television screens. We made an interesting caravan traveling down the highway or camping at a local campground.

Since I was up to my eyeballs in the everyday work of the ride, it did not dawn on me why morale was still so low.

Bob and Bea had left the ride back in Missouri and would catch up with us again in West Virginia. Brad and I had aired our differences in Oklahoma and had come to some understanding; we were now voicing our opinions early on rather than letting our concerns build up. Although this was working, it felt at times as though we were just going through the motions. I wasn't sure the team was going to hold together. We were all committed, but we were no longer enjoying the event.

Of course, it was grueling--early 4:00 AM mornings, bad weather, and a demanding schedule of appearances and riding. It became apparent to me that, if we were going to finish, we had to begin having some fun or at least smiling as though we were. And that is the conclusion I came to while sitting in my trailer on September 14th.

It was raining, my roof was leaking, and my back end was so sore that I could not sit upright. I was not happy. We'd been coasting. We were now comfortable at 22-25 miles per day, but we were losing ground and needed to ride more each day in order to finish in October. Brad and I both knew this, but neither of us made an attempt to suggest that we pick up the pace.

It was my problem. I was the push behind the ride and I was allowing us to coast. I may have been justifying it to myself as an opportunity to pull together some energy for that last big push. But, more likely, my subconscious was saying: "Take it easy, relax." My body was really hurting and it was all I could do to get into the saddle each day. My enthusiasm was waning. I was not pushing in the way I had been for the last 2300 miles.

This attitude was contagious. It was less apparent to everyone else that the low mileage we were doing was putting our mid-October finish in jeopardy. I realized I was somewhat to blame for the low morale, so I made a conscious decision to remedy the situation and make a concerted effort to improve morale. Any change had to start with me.

On September 14th, therefore, I made a decision to pump up the mileage, perk up, smile and show some enthusiasm. Not all at once, but gradually over the next 10 days; we knew each other too well, and a "cheerleader" change would have been much too obvious. But it worked. Gradually, we started pulling together better.

We rode some 35-and-40 mile days back to back in the next 15 days. My physical condition began to improve, and the fund-raisers were still tiring but fun. These back-to-back long-mileage days put us on target for a mid-October finish.

The day after I made the decision to try to boost morale, we decided to regroup for the next organizational and logistics nightmare. We had three more fund-raisers and media events to attend and we were about 200 miles, or a week and a half, behind schedule. We were scheduled to be riding through Ohio and West Virginia in late September. With this in mind, Francesca had set up promotional events in Athens, Ohio, Harrisburg, Pennsylvania, and McLean, Virginia.

If we were on schedule this would have put us in Athens in time for these events, and then allowed us to trailer one horse up to Harrisburg from our route in West Virginia as we did in St. Louis. But we weren't on schedule. We needed to attend the events and not lose riding time, but we were still in Indiana. Trailering back and forth each day to Athens and then Harrisburg would have taken extra hours, tiring the team and losing precious riding time.

We conferred with the Rainforest Action Network. After some discussion, we decided to skip the Indiana section for now and do it later. Instead, we would trailer up to Athens and spend nine days there, using my father's home in Athens as a base camp. Athens was right on our route. By following this plan we could ride all of the Ohio route and a good portion of West Virginia. At the same time we would attend the events in Athens and have a shorter trailer ride to the Harrisburg fund-raiser as well. At the end of this nine-day stretch, we would then trailer back into Indiana to pick up the 220-mile stretch we had just leap frogged over.

This new plan enabled us to ride all of the route without losing time and still attend the events. Operating out of our base camp in Athens, we would ride each morning and then trailer back to my father's place and be available to attend various events. Each morning we would trailer out to our stopping point from the previous day and continue riding toward and eventually past Athens into West Virginia. This worked; during that stretch, September 15-24, we rode all of the Ohio route and a big chunk of the West Virginia route and were still able to attend the fund-raiser in Harrisburg. On the 24th we returned to our stopping point in Indiana and continued riding east. It took us eight days to ride the stretch from Huntingbird, Indiana, to just east of Cincinnati.

The coasting we did in Indiana just prior to this leap frog was very important. It allowed us to regroup and pull some energy together for what I would call "our last big hill"--the heavy schedule of riding and performing at fund-raisers before our stretch to the finish. But it was great having a base camp for nine days.

After we completed the route in Ohio and finished the fund-raising events in Athens and Harrisburg, it was a very depressing trailer ride back west to Indiana to pick up that 220--mile stretch we jumped over. It was offset eight days later, though, by the exhilaration we all felt as we completed the stretch in Indiana and then drove all the way through Ohio and into West Virginia. Driving over the route we just rode two weeks before was great--a real sense of accomplishment. That was the first time in the ride that we had had a chance to retrace our steps after riding a stretch.

The following article came out in the editorial section of an Ohio paper. I believe it captures the essence of what we were trying to accomplish.

We also had some good news during this stretch. CNN had, in fact, picked up the ride and did two Earth Matters segments on our event. We also had some news that Willard Scott, the weather man on Good Morning America, was interested in our ride and might be able to meet us on the road to telecast a weather report. It would have been appropriate as the tail end of this segment caught the tail end of Hurricane Hugo. Those two days were not fun riding.

How did we get Mr. Scott's attention? Al-Marah had provided several thousand postcards of Sweet William and me so that we could mail these out from the road to people who might be interested. We had about 3000 of these left, so in our monthly newsletter from the road we enclosed a self-addressed card to Willard Scott. Our letter from the road at that point was going to about 2200 people we had met along the way plus many others. Upon receiving the card these people

The
Athens
NEWS

-Established 1977.-

-Publisher-
Bruce Mitchell

-Editor-
Terry Smith

-Advertising Manager-
Sherrie Bossart

-Graphics Editor-
Mary Conklin

-Photo Editor-
Stan Kokotajlo

-Writers-
David Bruce
Jim Phillips
Tracy Lassiter
Christine Nielsen
Jeff Chappell
Corinne Colbert
Kevin Walzer
Christina Nuckols

-Photographers-
Martha Rial
Ray Saviciunas
Cie Stroud
Kevin Casey

OPINION

Now & Again

Rain forest rider opens some eyes

By Jeff Chappell
Athens NEWS Writer

I've often been criticized for being a cynical person. Friends, ex-girlfriends, parents, relatives, co-workers — I've heard it from every corner, and with just cause. They're right. From religion to relationships, my views are pretty grim compared to most.

But like most journalists I also have a streak of idealism — the world really sucks and I'm out to change it. Yet, in the daily grind of classes and holding down two jobs, sometimes I lose sight of it.

Occasionally, though, something happens to remind me why I got into journalism — why I hold two jobs on top of classes and worry about deadlines and gripe about sources and column inches. One of these somethings happened Sunday morning when I met Lucian Spataro.

As I stood on the berm of the Appalachian Highway on that cool, breezy morning and talked with this guy astride his white Arabian horse, I was taken by a sense of urgency in his voice as he spoke of the rain forests. My idealistic streak, which had lain dormant for a long time, came alive.

It came alive with good reason. This guy had taken a year — a *whole damned year!* — off from his life to ride across America to raise awareness of a problem that few people know much about but which most likely will determine the course of the world. Spataro's not making any money at it; he hasn't even raised nearly the amount of money he wants to donate to the Rainforest Action Network.

Granted it's something he has always wanted to do, but how many people would allow a year's interruption in their lives for a worthy cause and then not gain anything?

Furthermore, most people who hear about Lucian Spataro will probably forget about him and

the plight of the rain forests by next month. (Here comes the cynicism!) They'll talk about it for a day or two at work or at dinner and then forget about it, as apathy takes over; it's just another problem the media blows out of proportion.

But perhaps a few people across the nation will have had their eyes opened. Perhaps even this column will incite someone to pay more attention to this issue and others.

Even if it's only one person, that would be worth it. It would make it worthwhile sacrificing a chance to party on Saturday night and awaking early Sunday — all to talk to Lucian Spataro on a cold, dreary morning. I can't speak for Lucian but I think he would agree that it was worthwhile.

You may not get a chance to read this, Lucian, and our paths probably won't cross again. If not, I'm glad I met you, and thanks for the kick in the idealism. Good luck with your part in changing the world. I'm glad I could help.

The essence of what we are trying to accomplish.
Courtesy of Athens News / Jeff Chappell

83

were instructed to sign their name and write on the back where they were from and that their friends were riding across the United States to raise money and make the public aware of the rainforest issue. All of these cards were sent to Willard's office in New York.

However, Willard Scott also received a postcard at his home address in Virginia. As we were riding through Virginia, two supporters of our effort, Terry Dudis and Marie Ridder, had a fund-raiser for us. They invited Willard and his wife and sent this invitation to him on one of the postcards. He probably thought: "Oh my God, they found my home address." Anyway, it caught his eye, and he phoned in to Terry that he could not make it, but that he was happy we were finishing. I was disappointed, but this was quickly offset by the CNN piece.

The fund-raisers in Athens were really something. High attendance and the fact that it was my hometown made them special. Most importantly, the people who attended were sincerely interested in the issue. The mayor of Athens, Sara Hendricker, proclaimed it Rainforest Week and presented the Ride Across America team with a city proclamation. We had our first media event there at a place called the Dairy Barn, a restored dairy barn, formerly a part of the State Hospital farm and, now operating as a cultural arts center and meeting place in Athens. That evening the local ecology clubs put on a concert with local bands, and over 350 people attended.

The feature act was by the band Barefeet, in which my brother John played guitar. They are actually really good. It was the first time I had a chance to watch my brother in action and I was impressed. It gave me a little different perspective on John.

We are very different. He is 12 years younger than I am. That age difference means a lot--I mean, I somehow pictured him as still the little brother I used to pick on at home in his crib. He's grown quite a bit now and is taller and bigger than I am. So picking on him now is out of the question. Our age difference is the time I've been away from Athens, so seeing him really showed me how much time had elapsed since I left home.

John really didn't think much of my endeavor to ride a horse this far--at least, he didn't show that he did. But he did show an interest in the horses and always stood outside the house petting or just watching them. By now many things I do that are a bit out of line don't faze John much. I think he and other members of my family have come to accept that I periodically go off and do something crazy. I remember my first mountain climb for a Guinness Record scuba attempt at high altitude really put my mother and father in shock, but, over the years, they got used to activities like these.

My father worked hard setting up different fund-raisers and speaking engagements in Athens. He was very supportive and didn't question my motives or my decision to attempt the ride. I spoke to him off and on during the planning stages and we discussed the trade-offs of undertaking an event like this. I remember speaking to him about the personal and economic sacrifices. His comment was: "If you are going to do it, go all the way." He even promised to buy me dinner at Tucson's most exclusive restaurant, the Tack Room, when I finished the ride. Come to think of it, he still owes me that dinner.

I had been back in Athens for a day here and there in the last twelve years, but only to drop in and say "hi." I never had much time to spend and would quickly leave and head back to Tucson or California. As I was riding toward Athens, I recalled how, twenty years before, I rode into the town center with my friends and their horses to get something to eat at Woolworth's, or just rode up to the campus of Ohio University in an attempt to impress the 20-year-old college girls. We'd let them ride or give them a ride and talk about it for days.

I also remembered swimming across the Hocking river with my horse Tim and my last Athens horse, Buck. I bought both these horses from friends, John and Leo Sheridan, and I was hoping I might see Leo when I was in Athens. I had heard John died a couple of years ago, and I remembered him, not only as the person who sold me my horse, but someone I called if I needed to talk or just had a question about feed or grain or saddles. I rode by his farm almost every weekend for 10 years. He was also our school-bus driver and picked me up every morning at my bus stop. I remember thinking how much I would like to see John when I got back to Athens.

The last time I saw him was about five years ago, when I drove past his farm. He was mending a fence near the road and I stopped to say hello. We only talked for a few minutes because he had another person there, helping him on the fence. I said I would stop by later. I never got the chance. I really would have enjoyed talking with him about this ride.

The response from the Athens community in general was great. Even some of my older high school friends who were in town showed up at the fund-raisers. It was nice to see them again and they were very supportive. I was a little disappointed to find out that many of the high school friends, who I knew were still in town, didn't come. And some of the their parents who I had become very close to also didn't show up. I really wondered why and I still don't know. Maybe they didn't hear about the ride, but that was hardly possible because it covered the front page of all three Athens papers two days running. It was more likely that the speaking engagements were during weekdays and during working hours. For whatever reason, there were a lot of people who I thought might show up but didn't, and people I didn't expect to come, did. So it was a wash.

Looking back on my Athens years now, I kind of wonder if during all that time I overestimated or misunderstood those friendships. Nevertheless, the town brought back a lot of really nice old memories and I had fun staying there again.

Athens is a town with a character all its own. I remember coming back to Athens in the early 80's and finding a phone booth where you could still make ten-cent phone call. The city has many brick streets, and the main street of the town is about 400 yards long.

The town is perched up on top of a series of small hills and surrounded by the Hocking River. So it is much higher than the surrounding area. When I was a child, the Hocking River used to flood and the town would be surrounded by a moat.

Since that time, they built a by-pass that brings most of the traffic around the city. The U.S. Army Corp of Engineers rerouted the Hocking River so it doesn't flood the University and the streets and houses of Athens anymore.

The campus of Ohio University dominates the downtown area. It is the lifeblood of the community. Ohio University has about 18,000 students and the town doubles in population when school is in session. With all the college activities, Athens has enough to do to keep a youngster occupied and busy and in just enough trouble to keep life interesting, especially for parents.

The day after the reception at the Dairy Barn, my father set up several speaking engagements at local schools where the horses and the team members and I loved to go. Children are so sincere and so interesting to speak with, and so much older and more mature nowadays than I was at their age. I think their exposure at a young age to technology and the media have allowed them to grow and mature intellectually faster than my generation did. These kids are working on computers at the age when I was barely able to swing a bat and add and subtract.

The presentations went over very well and I think the horses enjoyed the attention from the children as much as we did. It was as if they knew they were the honored guests, and the kids had a chance to pet each one.

It was late in the day, September 17th, but Brad and I decided to go out for a last minute ride; we got in 12.5 miles. Every mile counted. The total that day: 39.5 miles. We did 27 in the morning and then the 12.5 that night. We were keeping up the pace and covering the distance in spite of the events we were scheduled to attend each day. These were very long days for us all. We would ride, trailer to an event that afternoon, trailer back to our route and ride some more, then back to our base camp and sleep. It was very demanding, but it was allowing us to chalk up the miles.

Along the miles of road I had ridden, I had seen many hundreds of billboards. These, like television ads, newspaper ads, and radio jingles, bombard the public to buy, buy, buy, consume, consume, consume. It seemed to me, looking at all those advertisements, that economic progress has brought on a consumption frenzy.

Soaring repair costs have encouraged us to become a "throw-away society." It is now cheaper, it seems, to throw away a radio or T.V. when it breaks than it is to have it repaired. We tend to buy a new automobile every few years rather than continue maintenance on the older one. Manufacturers build a life expectancy or planned obsolescence into various products, which allows the companies that sell these products to project new sales on this pre-planned life expectancy.

To a large extent, these companies determine when a product will fail and thus when we will need to replace or repair it. If the company prices the repair parts at a higher cost than replacing the product, the option to buy a new replacement becomes our best choice. By doing this, ongoing sales are ensured. Ad campaigns for automobiles stress the new model, new design and style. There are fewer incentives to keeping an older car when we are all told the advantages of driving the latest model.

Today we bear the consequences of a "throw-away society": accumulation of huge and unnecessary amounts of solid waste. We are literally burying ourselves in our own waste. There are not enough landfills to hold the staggering amounts produced every day in our cities. As a result, cities in the East pay trucks to haul garbage and solid wastes to landfills in the Midwest.

As I rode through my hometown of Athens, Ohio, local environmentalists and concerned citizens were trying to block the dumping of garbage from New York in Athens County. There were numerous articles and extensive media coverage about the issue. But a United States Supreme Court ruling states that garbage is a commodity, and states cannot refuse to take out-of-state waste. Therefore, the landfill operator is allowed to accept waste from New York as long as the out-of-state trucks continue to pay the nominal dumping charges.

Some cities have tried to solve the solid waste problem by using garbage as fuel for incinerators designed to generate heat and energy. I learned that Columbus, Ohio, has been using an incinerator for several years. People familiar with this system told me that on many days you can smell the incinerator several miles away. So it may solve the immediate problem of the solid waste, but the resulting air pollution may cause greater problems.

The solution to solid waste disposal with the most promise is recycling. If we can recycle more and consume less, many of the recycled materials could become solid resources for industry and consumers as well.

I was impressed with the progress Athens had made in the collection of recycled material. The program they have established could be a model for many small towns across America. It is called the Athens Curbside Recycling Program. A volunteer group (SORT), the health department and a local sheltered workshop are all working together with a grant from the Ohio Department of Natural Resources. They have curbside pick-up twice weekly, and accept eleven recyclable items: (1) newsprint, (2) glass, (3) aluminum cans, (4) tin/steel cans, (5)aluminum scrap, (6) office paper, (7) computer paper, (8)computer cards/manilla folders, (9) cardboard, (10) pasteboard, and (11) grocery

Lucian speaks to a crowd at the Dairy Barn in Athens, Ohio.
Courtesy of Cie Stroud

sacks. As we were using my father's home as a base camp, I had the opportunity to see the response on recycling day. Almost every driveway on Strathmore Boulevard was piled high with bundles of newspapers, sacks of aluminum cans, cardboard and glass.

The recycling program in Athens not only cuts down on the amount of solid waste but it also provides employment for several people and income after the recycled items are sold. I spoke to Tom O'Grady, the brainchild behind the Athens Recycling program, and found that the program is growing quickly. In 1989 the recycling program in Athens processed 1.5 million pounds of material. In the first 6 months of 1990 alone the center did over 1.3 million pounds.

If Athens can do it and it is successful on this smaller scale, larger towns should be able to implement an effective system and capture those valuable recyclables materials. In Athens it took some strong leadership locally and several small grants to get started, but now it's nice to see neighbors outdoing neighbors as they place their recyclables on the curb every other week.

I read an article by David Morris of the Washington-based Institute for Local Self Reliance in a book called THE STATE OF THE WORLD 1987. He said something which I think expresses the problem well: "A city the size of San Francisco disposes of more aluminum than is produced by a small bauxite mine, more copper than a medium copper mine, and more paper than a good sized timber stand. San Francisco is a mine. The question is how to mine it most effectively and how to get the maximum value from the collected material."

Producing aluminum from recycled cans instead of bauxite cuts energy usage and air pollution by 95 percent. Making paper from recycled waste paper instead of virgin timber not only saves valuable forests, it also reduces the energy used per ton to produce that paper by 75 percent and requires less than half as much water. A large portion of what we consume is fossil fuel. By consuming less and recycling more, we can slow the production of carbon dioxide. Recycling can reduce the build-up of carbon dioxide in the atmosphere as we save valuable natural resources, consume less energy, and reduce significantly the solid waste problem.

Many cities that I traveled through showed little evidence of any attempt to recycle. People are often hampered by the "used goods mentality," and used products, cars for example, hold very little appeal to affluent Americans. Contrast this attitude with our attitude toward used currency. No one objects to handling or using recycled money. We must convince people that used products and recycling have value, just like used money.

In an effort to market most products, packaging has become a national obsession. Research tells us what colors to use and how to design the package to catch the consumer's eye. For example, with regard to food products, it seems that more time is spent on packaging and marketing than on assuring the consumer that what is inside is,

A reclaimed hillside in Athens, before and after.
Courtesy of Tom O'Grady, Athens Recycling Program

90

in fact, nutritious. We seem to be paying more for the package that the products come in than for the product itself. Why is this happening? Is this because the consumer is convinced that a better-looking package means a better product?

On one occasion, as I discarded my foam package, the plastic covering of my plastic fork, my plastic fork and my styrofoam cup in the trash bin at McDonald's (yes, Ride Across America stopped at Mc-Donald's), I noticed a beautiful placemat. It had a colored photograph of the earth with the title: "The Environment: What in the World is McDonald's doing about it?" Then it lists the following:

1) Recycled paper: Happy meal boxes, napkins, tray liners, and many other items are made of recycled paper.

2) Recycled plastics: Many McDonald's provide two trash bins, one for recycling plastic and one for other trash.

3) Foam packaging: McDonald's has removed chlorofluorcarbons from its polystyrene packaging.

4) Rainforests: McDonald's does not, has not and will not purchase beef from rainforest or recently deforested rainforest land.

5) Source reduction: McDonald's is eliminating much of its packaging and shipping material.

If what they say is true, this is quite an accomplishment and a very aggressive approach. However, the McDonald's I was in at the time did not have two bins and was not recycling plastic. I also know that in the past McDonald's and the fast food chains, specifically Burger King, have bought rainforest beef. The country of origin of various meat products is very hard to determine and rainforest beef is often mixed with 51 percent domestic beef and then declared domestic.

Apart from the issue of waste, litter is still a big problem in the United States. As I rode along the highways and rural roads I was often knee-deep in trash. We always had to be very careful of glass fragments along the sides of roads, and, in some places, for example in California, this was a major concern. I couldn't help wishing we were back in the days of refundable bottles. If people could get money back on their glass bottles, perhaps they would be less inclined to throw them away.

On September 19th--still on the Ohio leg--I rode 27 miles in the rain. I crossed the Ohio river at Parkersburg, West Virginia, and rode another 20 miles into West Virginia. We were now on U.S. Route 50. I planned to ride this all the way to the coast. Brad picked us up and we drove back to Athens to shower and change. Then we drove the 380 miles to Harrisburg, Pennsylvania, for the scheduled fund-raiser. Brad and I got in real late, about 10:00 PM, and met Char Magarro, RAN's East Coast coordinator who was hosting the event. We set up the pen for March Along in Char's backyard and crashed. We were beat.

The next day we got up early and drove down into Harrisburg to meet 50 other riders. March Along and I, and Brad--on a borrowed

Lucian and Sea Ruler in Athens riding toward West Virginia

horse named Hi Windsong--led a parade of about 150 people and horses through downtown Harrisburg and into the state capitol of Pennsylvania. We met representatives from the governor's office and had a rally on the steps of the capitol. Various people spoke on Pennsylvania's environmental commitment.

Randy Hayes, the director of the Rainforest Action Network, flew in to speak as well. He was just in from New York and had been at a meeting with United Nations Secretary General Xavier Perez de Cuellar. At that meeting, he had presented a worldwide petition with 3.5 million signatures. They brought the petitions into the United Nations building in 100 grocery carts.

The petitions included 600 thumbprints from natives living in the Penan Rainforest of the southeast Asian nation of Borneo--under attack from Japanese and United States logging interests. The petition called for a United Nations special session on the rainforest issue. Randy was pleased with the results and spoke to the crowd about the importance of grass roots groups like the Rainforest Action Committee of Harrisburg. These groups, Randy said, were needed to mobilize the public and put pressure on politicians and corporations. A letter writing campaign to Burger King caused them to cancel more than $35 million dollars in orders for Brazilian beef, he said.

After speaking, I was presented with a letter from the governor of Pennsylvania, Robert P. Casey, that endorsed and supported our efforts. Despite the long drive to Harrisburg and the pressure it had put on our schedule, we were pleased with the results. We had substantial television and newspaper coverage. My uncle, Carl Spataro, who lives in Harrisburg, took a day off from work to walk in the parade as well. I had the opportunity later that evening and the next day to visit with both my Aunt and Uncle. I had not seen them in over 20 years.

The most enjoyable part of that event was the party that Char had at her place that evening for all of the participants in the parade. Brad got a chance to play some basketball with Ona, Char's daughter. He lost! She was quite an athlete.

We woke up early the next day, the 21st of September, to drive down into Gettysburg for another round of fund-raisers. We thanked Char and her daughter Ona for their help in organizing the parade and we took off with the understanding that they would meet up with us again at the finish. We got to Gettysburg only to find that our fund-raisers had all been canceled as a result of bad weather related to Hurricane Hugo. Brad and I spent the night in Gettysburg and then drove back to Athens the next day. The three-day break from riding was great. We got back to Athens fairly fresh and ready to hit the road again.

On September 23rd we rode 25 miles farther into West Virginia and then drove back to Athens. That evening we had a farrier come out and look at both horses, reset the shoes and replace the Easy Boots on them. After that, we broke camp that evening at my father's place and

Parade in Harrisburg, PA riding to meet Governor Casey.
Courtesy of Patriot News/Bob Levy

COMMONWEALTH OF PENNSYLVANIA
OFFICE OF THE GOVERNOR
HARRISBURG

GREETINGS:

As Governor, I welcome you to our Commonwealth and extend congratulations on your efforts to increase America's environmental awareness through Ride Across America.

In Pennsylvania, we are striving to save our environment through investing in clean water, recycling and toxic waste cleanup.

Our legacy as a state and as a people rests on our ability to clean up the environment. Our quality of life depends on the standards we set for ourselves and future generations. Just as we share great expectations for our children, so do we share the responsibility of giving them a better world.

Three of the major concerns we face as a world are massive deforestation, ozone depletion and global warming.

Our rainforests provide us with 25 percent of all medicines in United States pharmacies; they are also the single largest source of oxygen. But at the rate they are currently being destroyed, tropical rainforests will be gone by the year 2050.

We have a long way to go in our fight to repair the damage done to our resources, but through education and awareness, especially of our young people, we can rebuild the environment.

I support your efforts to raise environmental awareness.

Best wishes.

Robert P. Casey
Governor

Congratulatory letter from Governor Casey, presented on the steps of the Capital.

prepared for our trip back to Indiana to pick up the 220 mile stretch we jumped over. We got down into Indiana at about 4:00 PM on the 24th, set up camp and went to bed. I slept straight through till 6:00 AM the next day. We had overslept for the first time on the ride. This showed us how tired we all were from the last nine days of riding and fund-raising.

During the next stretch, I rode 29.2 miles on the 25th; 41.3 on the 26th with two horses; 36 miles on two horses on the 27th; 18.5 on the 28th; 31.3 miles on Sea Ruler on the 29th; 25.2 miles on two horses on the 30th; 22.5 on the 1st of October; and 23 miles on the 2nd of October. We were now east of Cincinnati.

Our route crossed the Ohio River at Madison, Indiana. I then rode into northern Kentucky staying south of Cincinnati, crossed the Ohio River again and then rode up east of Cincinnati to State Highway 32. At this point we met up with the previously completed Ohio stretch. Over that last stretch in Indiana, we averaged 28.4 miles per day, our best stretch yet. So Indiana did not turn out to be such a bad state after all.

To give you a first-hand account of a non-member who worked with us for three days, I have included some extracts of an unpublished version of photographer Cie Stroud's account during the Kentucky and Ohio stretch. She is a photographer from Ohio University, now working in New York. She prepared the following piece, with pictures, for a freelance article. Some of the pictures were eventually published, but not the article. I've also included some of the pictures to go with it.

"I'll call in a couple of days and let you know where we are," he said. Friday the 29th of September: 5:45 AM Lucian telephones. "I thought you said you got up early," he says.

"I do, but..." 5:45 AM is 15 or 20 minutes short of my wake-up threshold.

"We're in Cincinnati," he says. Good grief. I hear that Cincinnati is a three-or four-hour drive. I'll have to leave this afternoon to get enough material for a picture storyboard for class. "So exactly where, Lucian?" I say.

"Yeah, so we're in Cincinnati, and we are about to go out riding," he says.

Just great, I think to myself, he's not awake either and he is going to get himself killed and me lost. "WHERE Lucian?"

"At the Batavia State Park. There's a big lake, have you got a map?" I look at my Ohio map hanging over the telephone. "Batavia exists--without a state park, but there is a big lake at Logan State Park--good enough." "Loop A, we're in loop A. Go in the park at the east gate," he says.

"Okay, see you tonight around seven," I say and crawl back into bed.

Basically, what the sign at the closed ranger station says is "If all else fails, call the sheriff." So I do. I have been driving the

roads from the east gate of the Logan State Park for what seems an hour. I've even got a glimpse of the "big lake" but no sign of Lucian. It is now pitch black out and I am ready to call it a day.

"I'm looking for Lucian Spataro, he's riding a horse across the States," I tell the operator at the Sheriff's department. "He says he is in loop A." Voices at the other end of the line from my cold pay phone confer, "What's his name? And he's doing what?" They must think I'm loony, I think to myself. Several minutes later and several pounds of quarters lighter I'm told, "stay where you are. We'll send an officer to escort you there." Thirty minutes later, I am following a patrol car to the camp-sites. Suddenly the officer slows, pulls to the side of the unmarked lit road and leans out the window to talk to someone walking along the road in the dark. It's Lucian.
From the light in the patrol car I see the officer shake his thumb over his shoulder at me and Lucian laughs. Lucian gets into my car. "I thought you weren't going to make it," he says cautious-ly.
I look at him out of the corner of my eye. "For someone riding a horse across the States you sure have a lousy sense of direction, Lucian," I say. He pauses for a second, then laughs.

Rise and shine is cold, painful, and in what seems the dead of night. Brad Bradin, the trainer accompanying the Ride, shines a flashlight in on Lucian. Lucian groans. It's around 6:00 AM. Lucian pours some cereal in a bowl and opens the fridge for some milk. In the fridge are several vials of medicine for the horses and a lonely quart of milk. Lucian quietly eats the bowl of cereal and hops out of the trailer. In the dark, he and Brad load March Along into the trailer-adapted back of Lucian's camper, hook up the camper to the truck and pull out of the park.
I follow in my car, cameras loaded. A light above March Along glowing through the back windows of the trailer is the only light I see as the camper drives through a small town, across a set of railroad tracks, and through the fog over the highway to the on ramp for route 32. Dawn breaks as the trailer pulls to the side of the road just past the junction with 270.
Brad unloads March Along, hands him to Lucian and prepares the tack. I feel myself tense from the sound of the cars whiz-zing by, just feet away. March Along turns his head away from Lucian, takes two or three glances at the surroundings, blinks and turns to Brad who then bridles him. The blanket comes off next and Lucian takes a good look over March Along as Brad brushes down the Arabian.
Once March Along is saddled up, horse and rider cross the divided highway to ride east along the shoulder. Neither one makes much effort to cross quickly between the pairs of oncoming headlights. I turn to find Brad has already packed up and is preparing to return to the campsite. It seems business as

usual. I decide to follow Lucian in my car. . . .

I let the two ride past and then photograph the small world of horse and rider where the sound of the hooves striking the pavement endures after the cars and trucks that appear from the fog behind roar by and drive off and disappear again into the fog. . . .

Back at camp Brad and Joyce are sipping coffee in their camper. I ask how they spend their time while Lucian rides. The remaining horse they bathe and groom, there's grocery shopping to do, camping arrangements to make and good hay and grain to find. Brad adds that he reads a lot of books. I laugh. I ask how they find Lucian in this stage of the ride.

"That boy," says Joyce, " I worry about him getting seriously hurt. His reactions aren't as quick, he's tired and it's dangerous out on that road." She shakes her head.

Brad says: "Mr. Spataro is getting the job done." Lucian hasn't skipped any miles in the ride. "He's got too much integrity to do that," says Brad. . . .

The sun dries up the fog and I take a seat at the picnic table between the campers and watch March Along. Brad comes out to look over the Arabian and takes a seat at the picnic table. Three boys walking along the road on the far side of the pens stop to look at the fair Arabian standing at attention, watching their every move.

March Along has heard them coming. "That's a pretty horse, Mister," says the outspoken boy.

"Can I have him?" the quiet one asks seriously.

"He's not for sale," replies Brad. . . .

"No," Brad starts, "he (Lucian) is not a horseman. He's a rider. I'm here to look after the horses and he's here to make the ride. It's a

team . . . It's about that time," says Brad, and he and I drive out to the day's endpoint. Brad estimates the time it will take the pair to arrive at the endpoints by a three-and-a-half-mile-an-hour pace. . . .

March Along announces our return with deafening whinnies. He paces and throws his head in the air. In all my years of riding I have never heard or seen such a commotion when two horses are reunited. What camaraderie! March Along's greetings brighten the end to the day's long ride.

After some difficulty in parking the monstrous camper, and once Sea Ruler is in his pen and the two Arabians are put nose to nose, March Along becomes quiet and the two horses eagerly begin to eat their grain. They stop suddenly to raise their heads and ears to listen to the park's trail horses nearby. I hear nothing but am fascinated by their attention and smart stances. They pace back and forth in their pens for a minute, but are again arrested by what they hear. Their ears turn and twist and their eyes are wide. I notice Brad, Joyce, and Lucian are captivated by the horses too.

Lucian, Sr. arrives sooner than we expected. "I saw the Logan

Park sign and took the chance that's what he meant," he says. I wish I had done the same. Lucian Sr. knows his son pretty well. While Brad and Lucian's father chat, I look through Lucian's kitchenette cupboards for a glass. In the cupboards are several cans of pineapple, a container of powder protein mix and an unopened jar of peanut butter. What does this guy eat? It's again about that time and Lucian's father, Brad and I pile into the truck and drive out to the day's endpoint--Measley Ridge Road. We pass Lucian still riding. Brad maneuvers the camper into a dead end just off the highway a few yards past Measley Ridge Road. The three of us talk as the rain blurs the once-wip- ed windshield. I ask Lucian's father what he thinks about his son's adventure. He says Lucian is a dedicated person and that's something he admires.

After nearly forty minutes someone says, "It sure is taking him a long time." Silence overcomes the cab. Brad turns on the wipers and clears the windshield. "You know, Brad," I say, "that last half mile or so is up-hill." It didn't occur to me before. "It's not a Measley ridge after all, is it?" says Brad. Several minutes later, in the grey scene before us appears the yellow rain suit.

Cie, in her essay, left out two very funny incidents that took place during her visit. On her first day with us when loading the trailer that first morning, we forgot to lock in, and as a result we drove about 10 feet with the trailer dragging in the bed of the truck, not too bad but loud enough to stop us and awaken Joyce in the next trailer. The next day when Brad was leaving to pick me up, he backed into my father's car and destroyed the door. Not a good two days. Our first accident on the trip.

We were a little nervous having a visiting journalist on the ride. It was funny how self-conscious we were after all those miles as an outsider recorded our ride in pictures and text. Usually a journalist might come in and take some staged picture or ask a few questions, but no one had lived with us for several days in an effort to captured the real ride 24 hours a day. It wasn't all that romantic; it was just hard work.

After riding on October 2, we broke camp and drove across Ohio and into West Virginia driving across the route we had just ridden. We were now at a base camp in Grafton, West Virginia. We would ride the stretch east and west of Grafton and then on into Virginia. It was October 3rd and the leaves were just beginning to change color. It was cool at night. The rain had stopped.

Athens had been a turning point. We'd had some fun, but achieved a lot, too. I had the chance to go home for a little while and spend some time with my family. And the town brought back some good memories. But there was one incident in Athens that was not so good.

East of Athens on highway 33, I rounded a bend in the road and found a four-car collision that must have happened only seconds before. There was one man trying to both direct traffic and pull people from the cars. Two cars were overturned and the other was on its side. This was not a pretty sight as there were probably a total of ten people in the four cars.

I quickly dismounted and began directing traffic to allow the other man to pull people out of the car. He was overwhelmed, so I tied Ruler up and began to help. We were both in way over our heads and I was inclined to leave several of the people in the cars until more qualified help could arrive. I didn't want to move anyone without the proper equipment. I convinced the man to concentrate with me on those who we could reach and who could definitely move without harm.

Just as we began to assist these people, several ambulances pulled up. I then went back to directing traffic and soon thereafter was relieved of this duty by a police officer. I didn't see the accident so I couldn't answer any questions. With nothing else to do, Ruler and I rode on. About 20 minutes later, a police officer drove by and stopped to say thanks for the help. He said there were ten people in the accident, and the person who was working with me was also involved. It seemed he may have been the cause of the pile-up. Three people were okay and six were in the hospital, two seriously injured.

About 5 minutes after that my father pulled up, clearly shaken. I think he thought I was in the accident and drove out to check. He was relieved to find out that we were okay and still riding toward West Virginia. He took some pictures and went back to Athens. Oh, yes, he drove out to bring me some inserts for my running shoes, he said. A 80-mile drive round trip for a $1.00 pair of inserts. I hope I am as committed and supportive of my children as my parents have been to me.

On a cold and wet morning, March Along and Lucian riding east in Ohio on State Highway 32.
Courtesy of Cic Stroud

8

THE FINAL STRETCH, THE APPLE CART AND THE FINISH

West Virginia, Virginia, Washington, D.C. and Maryland

Being in Grafton, West Virginia, is a hell of a lot easier than getting there. This is one difficult town to find and maneuver around. Grafton is situated at an elevation of about 1200 feet among very craggy mountains. I do not know how else to describe the terrain but to simply say that it is rough. It reminds me a lot of the mountains coming out of Albuquerque--very sharp and deep. Plenty of tree-lined valleys, steep hills and clear cold streams. The horses and I drank out of the smaller streams along the road.

I had heard that there were many caves in the area. It made sense: I could see many high plateaus and ridges that appeared to slope in all directions at once. These were not gradual in all cases. Instead, many of the slopes were steep, and even precipitous. There were many rock formations and frequent vertical and overhanging cliffs. As we rode through this area we rode up and down these ridges and very seldom were we on level terrain.

Fall had descended upon the Appalachian Mountains and the trees were beginning to change color. Previous logging and farming have contributed to a great diversity of the vegetation in this area. I saw primarily white oak, both red and sugar maple, shag bark hickory, black oak, beech, and walnut. Most of these trees were located along the ridges and slopes and they changed colors at various times in the fall. The view of these ridges was often like a rainbow and, as we rode through the area, the rainbow changes as the terrain and the vegetation change. There were also many deciduous shrubs and smaller understory trees interspersed throughout--redbud, sassafras, flowering dogwood, apple, and maple. I saw a lot of paw paw, an edible fruit, and huckleberry and spice bushes.

The smell in the fall was overwhelming. The sassafras, apple, and paw paw and the cool clear air and cool clean water dazed all my senses--touch, smell, taste, sight, hearing. Everything was in razor-sharp focus. The deeper I breathed in, the clearer it became.

We usually traveled in a caravan when we drove to our next base camp, but going into Grafton we ran into a dense fog bank and got separated. We had agreed to meet in the Four Corners Cafe in case we got lost.

When I got to the cafe, I discovered that it was closed for the night. I asked for directions to the park and had no problem finding it. Brad and Joyce came in about one hour behind me and did the same--found Four Corners closed and went to the same gas station for directions. They were given the same directions I was given. The following excerpt is out of Joyce and Brad's journal:

"We took off with our directions and did real well for a while. The lady just forgot to tell us we'd have to go about 3 miles out of town; part of this was on a one-way street. We went to the end of this street, which turned into a very narrow two-way street or road. We figured we were wrong, so managed to get turned around and headed back the way we'd come. Well, we forgot to make one turn and found ourselves headed out of town on another road. Finally we came to a corner and Brad stopped. Some lady started to go around us, and Brad got out of the car and stopped her and told her our problem. She was a doll. She said to follow her and she'd take us there. We found another cubby hole and got turned around and followed her. She led us right back to that little narrow one-way street. She started up it. Brad and I figured she didn't know anymore than we did, so we decided to turn another direction. She stopped quickly, so Brad did too. Both got out and met in the middle of the intersection. This lady shook her finger at Brad and said, "Young man, I told you to follow me and I'd take you to the park." Brad said, "yes ma'am," and came back, and got the truck backed up to follow her. She took us straight to the park. When we arrived at the entrance, there sat Lucian waiting. It was now 12:30 AM and we could not see the campsites, so we just pulled our trailers into a tight circle, unloaded the horses, set up the pens with food and water and hit the bed."

When Brad told me this the next day, I laughed for an hour straight as I pictured this confrontation on a narrow road at midnight. I visualized Brad, a 72-year-old who didn't look 50, standing in front of this lady who was not a day past 50, and her shaking her finger at him calling him "young man." Also, the rigs, truck, and trailer that Brad was driving were over 40 feet long and my rig was well over 55 feet long. Both were very difficult to move in tight places.

We stayed at the Grafton city park, located just east and south of the town and situated just under the Tygart Lake dam. I understand this dam is the largest cement dam east of the Mississippi, with a solid cement base 200-feet wide. The city park sprawls along the river, which seems to originate below the dam. Getting to the park with our trailers and horses on the small one-way streets and narrow two-lane roads was no piece of cake for me, and it was, as Brad said, a very humbling experience.

Before 1960 Grafton was a glass producing town, with the Hazel Latis Glass Company as a major business entity. In the 30's, 40's and 50's, it was also a railroad switching and repair center for the B & O and then later the CSX railroad companies. The rail and glass industries were the principle employers in the valley.

All of the homes and some of the businesses are propped up on the hillsides or set down in the valley bottom. Many narrow one-and two-way streets meander around the residential areas and then into the main part of town, connecting the outlying areas in a roundabout way with the downtown area. For someone not familiar with the city and the one-way streets that seem to go on forever, it can be a dizzying experience.

Residents claim that Grafton is the final resting place for the first Yankee buried in the Civil War, T. Bailey Brown. Grafton is also the location of the first organized observance of Mother's Day, which took place in the Andrews Methodist/Episcopal Church. There, on May 10, 1908, Anna Jarvis led the first Mother's Day service ever held. They no longer hold regular services each Sunday in the church, but still hold Mother's Day services each year.

Bob and Bea got in about 5:00 PM on October 3rd. Brad and I were still out riding, so Joyce took some time to tell of our experiences during the last three weeks. She really enjoyed telling them about Brad and the woman who gave him directions the night before. It was good to have Bob and Bea back on the ride and with us for the final stretch. We all decided to go out that evening for dinner at the Four Corners Cafe, appropriately named as it sits at the juncture of Route 50 and 119, forming four corners. There I ate the best food east of the Mississippi and the best hot apple pie and homemade ice cream of my lifetime, with the exception of my mother's apple pie, of course.

On October 5th I rode through Grafton and actually completed my ride that day just beyond the Four Corners restaurant. As I was riding into the outskirts of town, Brad pulled up next to me and told me to stop. So I did, and found out that just around the bend, in front of a small cemetery and war memorial, was the site of a most unforgettable accident.

Two months before, a young lady named Claudia Von Ostwalden and her horse, Max, were traveling west along this same stretch until they were struck by a truck driven by the manager of a dealership in Grafton. Claudia was uninjured, but the horse could not go on. This horse and rider team were attempting to set a record by crossing the United States on horseback.

I found out later that the young lady was, in fact, trying to race us across the United States. From what I understand, she had seen an article in a magazine about our ride and had left the east coast soon after we left the west coast. I estimated by her pace that she rode 350 miles during the same time period we covered 1100 miles. I also found out later that she rode through Athens, Ohio, on her second horse, Sport, while the first horse was still in Grafton recovering from the accident.

Apparently she stopped somewhere just shy of the Texas border--her timing was off. She wanted to reach Oregon in September and she was still in Ohio in late July.

While doing my research for our ride, I found that our chances for success would be much better if we rode west to east, primarily for two reasons.

First, I knew the riding would be toughest, physically and psychologically, out west. I also knew that adrenaline and energy early in the event would carry us over this physical and psychological hurdle. The last thing I wanted was to see, with ebbing energy and unfocused eyes, was thousands of miles and countless horizons still to go. So going east to west was out. I knew we would need, toward the end of our journey, the moral support, as well as the additional stimulation, of the more populated eastern cities and towns.

The second reason was that it would be much easier to endure heat than cold. So, by riding east from California, we could pick up the very early warm spring days in California and Arizona, and this would give us basically five to six months of good riding. Going east to west we would not have that same luxury. It was still very cold in the east in May, but, importantly, riding east to west at our estimated pace could have put us in the west during October and November. Riding through those windswept stretches in New Mexico, Arizona, and California in the fall would not have been fun. I came to the conclusion that the only way to do it and catch the best of all three seasons was to begin in May in California and then ride as fast as possible, hoping to reach the east coast in late September or early October.

This young lady did just the reverse, and was riding much too slowly. At her pace I think she probably caught the first blast of fall weather somewhere just shy of Texas and decided to call it a ride. She still had the windiest and coldest stretches left to go. I remember how cold it was in the early mornings in May in the desert. I would not want to be riding through that area in the winter, or even in the fall.

Brad told me he had found out all about the young lady's accident as he was parked in front of the Ford Dealership looking for some water for the horses and some touch-up paint for the truck. He walked into the dealership with his boots and hat and, as was often the case, he was hit with a question or two about Arizona because of our license plate. He then started telling everyone within earshot about the ride and the rainforests (Brad was really getting the lingo down now on the rainforests).

Before he could go any further, he heard one guy say, "Well, that means we'll have to keep ol' Tom here off the roads until you and your rider get through town." It seems Brad was talking with the manager of the Ford dealership, who actually drove the truck that struck the young lady and her horse. So he got the real scoop from the "horse's mouth," as they say. The horse that got hit, by the way, was still in Grafton and doing fine.

Traveling down highway 50 in the fall from Clarksburg to Virginia and on into Washington, D.C., was a trip I will not soon forget. It was spectacular in the fall as the leaves were changing. As we drove at the break of day, we could see mist rising up from the many rivers and streams that parallel and cross the route. I saw wildlife at every turn.

Growing up in Ohio, I always told travelers that West Virginia was, and I believe still is, the most beautiful state east of the Mississippi. It is within a stone's throw of many major metropolitan areas all along the east coast, yet remains somehow primitive, isolated and unaffected. It is a place from a different time and reminds me a lot of the Ozarks. Small towns, with little more than a hardware store, cafe, and gas station, dot the route, each significant for a different reason.

The route was very historical, as we rode into Virginia, and brought up visions of the Civil War, Lincoln and the fight against slavery and oppression. There were landmarks everywhere identifying various battlegrounds and homes of gone but not forgotten heroes and citizens. The people in these small communities cling to the history of the area and speak of the various happenings as though it were only yesterday that these events occurred.

For me, it was a step back in time. Each town--Gormania, Red-house, Mt. Storm, and Junction--was named for very practical reasons. Junction for instance was a junction, a trail head of sorts years ago. Redhouse had a prominent red house near the center of town. Often the prominent family in the region got to name the town, sometimes for a family member, usually the father of the first clan to settle in the area. Very practical reasons and very practical people.

October 6th was a nasty day for riding. It was cold and sheets of wind and rain were blowing in every 15 minutes. Even March Along, who was usually able to adapt to bad weather, had his tail between his legs and back to the wind. Luckily we were riding with the wind and it was going to be a short day, only about 22 miles. This was all very steep terrain, high mountains and deep valleys, straight up and straight down. The road was very slippery. March Along had Easy Boots over his steel shoes only on his front feet, which helped as we were riding down the mountains but did not give us much traction going up. This particular stretch was even more treacherous as a result of one very large mountain that starts deep in the valley, climbs for four miles and then descends for six miles. The Cheat Mountain has 52 switchbacks on the way up.

A switchback, for those who are unfamiliar with the term, is a very tight switch in direction of a trail or road. The purpose is to make the climb easier so, instead of going straight up the mountain, the trail meanders back and forth, switching direction and climbing very slowly. As a result, it took us more than two hours to make the climb. The problem was compounded by the fact that U.S. Route 50 still continues to be a major truck route into the east coast and, on this particular day over this very narrow two-lane road in blinding rain, I counted 103 trucks in the ten-mile stretch up the mountain and down the other side. There are not many places on this narrow road for a horse and rider to move away from traffic. When one truck would pass another on a switchback, I could literally touch them, and did on many occasions.

Over the guard rail to our left or right was often just a sheer drop off, and the other side of the road offered nothing better, typically a sheer stone cliff rising up from the road. No place to go. Luckily, the trucks were going so slow up the mountain that they often saw us and made a significant effort to avoid coming too close. In such weather conditions, however, the truck drivers did not always see us and we had several very close encounters on this ten-mile stretch.

On October 7th, Bob and Bea caught up with Sea Ruler and me in the morning in Gormania. I needed to make a phone call to a Detroit radio station and took the opportunity to get some hot coffee, which I normally do not drink, and some fresh apple pie at the Country Cupboard Cafe. It was about 65 degrees outside and would eventually reach about 75 that day--a perfect day for riding. I made my phone call to Detroit and also made a phone call to Al-Marah in Tucson. With the time difference, it was about 8:00 AM in Tucson. I had already been up for seven hours.

The coffee wired me. As Bob said later, it was as "black as the bottom of the pot." It tasted good and warmed me up inside "real quick." In fact, I was on the phone with the radio station when it hit. That caffeine had me talking so fast that I was literally shaking. I had to stop the interview.

Later I spoke to a doctor about this. He said that the caffeine (which I was not used to) in combination with the small amount of food in my system and my puny body weight of 147 pounds, generated a response similar to an allergic reaction. Now, when I drink coffee, I drink it with ice and in a half water and half coffee mixture--cold iced coffee.

I rode 29 miles that day, most of it out of the saddle as a result of caffeine. I rode through a small corner of Maryland and then back into West Virginia. I wrote in my journal: "We are very close now and it is as if someone is dangling the carrot and just gave me the first nibble (Maryland)." I told the rest of the crew how I felt when I got back to camp. They all seemed to experience the same feeling.

On October 8th Sea Ruler and I climbed out of a four-mile-long valley and up onto a ridge about 1900 feet high. Somewhere on top of this ridge between Junction and Romney was a lookout that pointed south. The memorial read that Nancy Hanks, the mother of President Abraham Lincoln, was born on this ridge overlooking the valley, or something to that effect. (I did not write it all down in my journal, but I was impressed.)

From this high vantage point I could see nothing but tree-lined valley on and on into the horizon. It is not often in the east that one finds such a panoramic view. Out west I got very used to seeing the sun set or rise on a beautiful horizon and after a while I would take the scene for granted. But here in the east, after riding for months without a view like this, we stopped and sat for 20 minutes, looking over the magnificent landscape, then rode on.

For most of that day I was a little preoccupied with plans for our ride through Washington, D.C., and the final route to our finish. I had made several phone calls that day from the road in the small towns I rode through, trying to reach Charles Applebee of the Maryland Department of Transportation. I would reach the receptionist, and Applebee would be out. The secretary's first response: "Would you like to leave a message and a number where he can reach you?"

My response: "Tell him I'm the guy riding the horse across the United States and I'm 120 miles from Maryland and riding his way. I need him to clear a route for me to the beach."

"You must be kidding."

"No, I'm not. I'm dead serious. He will remember me. I spoke with him 6 months ago. Please tell Mr. Applebee to stay in his office tomorrow until 9:00 AM. I will call him then from my horse."

She must have thought I was loony toons.

For some reason, I put off defining and clearing the final route to the beach on the east coast until the last two weeks of the ride. I spoke with both the D.C. and the Maryland people a month before the ride began, but we could not put together a final route over the last 75 miles. I had justification for my procrastination on this very important final detail.

When I was in Tucson I did not know how we were going to ride through D.C. and then to the beach. On the west coast in L.A., I had a chance to peruse the route. On the east coast, 2300 miles away, I told myself (and I knew better), "We'll just play the last 125 miles by ear, add a little excitement." I did not know until about four days before the finish the exact route I would take in to the beach. Because of the literal maze of small streets and roads and small towns in this area, I thought we might just sneak on through, and this is actually what we did.

It worked until we got right in close to D.C. By and large it was horse country anyway, and we were on Route 50, which does not require permits, so in the rural areas between towns we did not stand out. But we still had to contend with all of the small towns and municipalities. I timed it so that I could ride through them all in the early morning or sometimes in the dark. At this point in the ride, I just did not have the energy, the time, nor the patience to deal with bureaucracy for the set of permits on the last 125-mile stretch. I remember saying to myself in Tucson, "I'll deal with this last stretch when we hit Virginia, and, when we make it that far, nothing will keep us from riding into the coast. We'll Rambo our way into the beach."

It turns out that last stretch did involve a little Rambo-ing and a little bit of bluffing, too. I rode every step of the way, but I did get stopped several times. In downtown Fredricksburg, I lied and told the police officer that I had a permit but that stopping me to find it would delay our ride that afternoon and probably put in jeopardy a media opportunity we had set up down the road. I then told the policemen our story and gave them all a brochure. In all cases, the police let us ride on through; in this case, with a police escort, no less. It made me wonder about all the time and energy I had put into getting the other 60-plus permits for the first 2800 miles. Had it even been necessary? Could I have just bluffed my way across the United States? Or were the officers so taken by our determination and confidence at this point that they assumed without question that we had permits, or we could not have gotten this far? I was betting on that.

Now, Washington, D.C., was a different story. Highway 50 goes right into D.C., and, rather than take the road right in to the Lincoln memorial, I rode through residential areas and even the Arlington cemetery, with a police escort of course. Bob Shepard began working with the D.C. police about five days before we were to ride through. We actually had only one permit for D.C., and we took that permit, and the encounters we had earlier with all of the police precincts we rode through approaching D.C., to develop some credibility. We asked them, basically, to call one another and coordinate our ride through the area, bootstrapping our credibility and implying that we obviously had a permit for each precinct through D.C. to the Maryland border. When using this strategy, the question of permits never came up. As they coordinated with one another, each precinct assumed that we must, in fact, have legitimate permits. So they just passed us from precinct to precinct.

We found out, as we were riding through Washington, that we actually needed a total of seven permits for the D.C. area, including one for the White House lawn. But we just kept on riding. We had some media coverage, and that helped to legitimize us and give us additional credibility. I've included a map of our detailed route through Washington and then around the Capitol and the White House and on down Pennsylvania Avenue. Our bluff didn't work with Mr. Applebee, (Maryland Dept. of Transportation), though. He knew I did not have a permit for Maryland, but he also knew that I knew I was not required to have a permit if I rode on any Maryland thoroughfare not listed as an interstate. He could do nothing about it.

By this time I had become very familiar with most of the state laws on this subject, and Mr. Applebee agreed to outline a route using rural roads and state four-lane highways on into Chesapeake Bay. He got the route approved in no time flat, and we were set, from Pennsylvania Avenue east of the capital to Chesapeake Beach, Maryland.

On October 8th our ride down Highway 50 continued; we were then camped at the Cherry Hill campground in Winchester, Virginia. I had come down off the ridge where Nancy Hanks was born and had ridden into a long valley. At the bottom, I had found a small hotel and made a phone call to Leslie Barclay to get directions to a small dinner she was having in our honor the next evening at Val Cook's in Washington, D.C.

Leslie and I talked on the phone for about 30 minutes. I had not spoken with her for several weeks, and she was pleased to learn we were going to make it. She confessed that back in New Mexico she and her husband Rucky had had their doubts. I found out later that Rucky had said he was sure we would make it. Leslie and Rucky had thrown a party for us in Santa Fe, New Mexico, to where we had trailered up from Albuquerque. I told Leslie that I was calling from the road and had Sea Ruler standing with me in front of the phone booth. She recalled the area; she had once done some fox hunting around there. I got the directions to Val Cook's home and told Leslie I would see her the next evening. That day I rode 28.3 miles on Sea Ruler.

October 9th was clear and cold. I had to scrape ice off the truck window that morning. No cloud cover at all. I'd learned that a clear night, when you can see the stars, is going to be a cold night no matter where you are and what season it is. Cloud cover seems to mitigate the cold. Humidity makes it seem, and I think actually be, warmer. I used the gas burners last night to heat the trailer. I slept great--must have been the propane leak sleeping again. I Rode 29 miles today, showered and changed clothes for the dinner in the evening. When I put my clothes on, I really looked skinny--not thin but skinny. Nothing fit and I must have looked like the bag monster.

I had Bea drop off my jacket, pants, and shirt at the dry cleaners in Winchester so I wouldn't smell as though I had just ridden in (which, I had, of course, but I didn't want to look and smell). How many people go to a party in Washington having just ridden in on a horse? I laughed as I realized that this could make for very interesting conversation at the party. I walked out of the trailer, and flash bulbs began going off. Bea and Joyce were having a heyday with me. Neither had

110

ever seen me dressed in anything other than running tights, boots, or jeans, with the exception of when we were in St. Louis, when I wore jeans and a jacket. Clad in a blue blazer, khaki pants, white shirt, red tie and a very nice tan that I really earned on the road, I left for the party.

After parking my pick-up truck between a Mercedes and a Jaguar, I noticed I still had some hay and horse manure in the back of the truck, I assumed that wouldn't bother anyone. I had a great time at the party and got a chance to talk about the ride and the rainforests. I met Val Cook's daughter, Diana, an avid rider, and some other very interesting people as well. I finally got back to my trailer park about 2:00 AM. I wrote in my journal that morning: "The next day is not going to be fun." I was right--It wasn't.

I always like to do my longest rides in a daze, when everything seems to fade by. On this day, October 10th, I had a 38-40 mile ride planned using two horses. I started out on Sea Ruler and rode 20 miles, and then Brad brought up March Along, so I put in another 20. I was fading fast on two-and-a-half hours' sleep, and then it started to rain. I still had 10 miles left to go and it was about 4:00 PM. I cantered March Along for three of the 10 and then began walking one mile and cantering a half mile, walk one, canter a half. This was miserable. To top it off, I did not have my rain gear with me, so I was soaked to the bone.

The excerpt from Bob's and Bea's journal that day reads like this:

"Tuesday, October 10, 1989, Bob and I took off after Bob made some phone calls for Lucian. Things are winding down now. We met up with Lucian about 20 miles out, he was beat, poor puppy! He was riding two horses today to cover 40 miles. We pulled into a driveway where Brad was waiting. Somehow we missed seeing that huge trailer on our way out. When Lucian rode up, Brad, Bob and Lucian looked at maps, planned timing and checked the route. March Along, who had been waiting in the trailer and was now saddled for the last 20-mile stretch that day, began nudging Lucian as if to say, "Lets get it going, it's going to be dark soon." Lucian asked Bob to make a few more phone calls for him. If Lucian could have his lap-top computer on the horse he would work on that, too. We left to make the phone calls and, while doing so, guess who rides up? Lucian had cantered the first two miles and caught us at the phone booth. Bob and Lucian talked on the two pay phones while I held March Along. We must have been the cause of a few near-fender-benders as we stood in front of the phones making calls with a horse. I took a picture. Hope it comes out. Phone calls finished, we went on to an all-day breakfast place and Lucian, down the road. We just love these small towns, the down home atmosphere, cautious but friendly people, slower pace. It's been a whole new life for us. We saw Lucian farther on down the road. He was on the phone again; he'll never finish today, 12 miles to go for the day. It's getting colder and will be dark soon. We don't like his riding in the dark, especially during rush hour. He doesn't seem bothered by it, though. The weather had turned really rotten by the time we returned to camp. Sea Ruler was acting up, bucking and kicking in the pen, nickering and stomping around. The wind was really blowing--maybe he smelled something. We had the new alfalfa delivered, Brad had the tire fixed on the trailer. They've gone through a few of those on this trip. Lucian called in and wanted some stew and another jacket; Brad took it out. It was dark now, and really cold and wet. Lucian was due in at 7:00 PM and, if he didn't arrive, Bob would have to cover the conference call Lucian had scheduled with Randy Hayes and Francesca Vietor in San Francisco. Three minutes off, and who rides in? Guess. He really made some time! After he made the call he came to our place and asked if he could stay with us. Of course we said yes. His place is so cold and he ran out of propane so the burners don't even work. He's putting everything into the finish; less important details are sliding. I think he wanted comfort and company. He ate the rest of Joyce's stew and then came over and we all watched THIRTY SOMETHING. (Through the eyes of Bob and Bea.)

I wrote in my journal that day: "This was the toughest day since Texas." I also wrote: "And this is the last tough day. I took a big chunk out of the carrot today. We are really going to make it."

Just before going to bed I did an interview with Dr. Bob Hieronimus, of the "Dr. Bob Show," on the American Radio Network. The talk show lasted 50 minutes, and I did it from a cold payphone in the Candy Hill Campground. We had seven call-ins on the rainforest topic. I was one of three on a panel answering questions about the ride and the rainforest.

At the end of the show, Dr. Bob asked the audience on the radio a question about the ride. If someone knew the answer they could call in and win a T-shirt and video. He asked what kind of horse I was riding across the U.S.A. One man called in from Ohio and said it was a white horse. Wrong, no prize. And then a lady called in from Florida and said they were Arabians, and she won. We finished the show and I hung up and went to bed. Long day.

October 11, 1989, I saddled up at a place called Atoka, Rectors crossroads where Mosby's rangers fought. John Mosby was known as the "Grey Ghost" in the Civil War. This stretch of Route 50 is known as the John Mosby Highway in memory of the rangers. Highway 50 is also an important commuter route to D.C. By chance I always seemed to catch some part of rush hour. This highway was like a large, long, four-lane parking lot in some places, so instead of riding the edge I would ride right down the road between traffic lanes. I would catch quite a bit of attention as I did this, and that gave me the opportunity to pass out brochures right off the horse as people would roll down their windows and ask me what in the hell I was doing out there. Great way to break the ice.

I rode through Upperville today. On the way in I passed an apple cart at a vegetable stand on the side of the road. The man was selling three different types of apples. I stopped and asked him If I could have an apple for my horse. I only had $.50 on me to make phone calls if necessary and I didn't want to spend it, so I told him I didn't have any money on me. He gave me two bruised apples from the back of the cart. I ate one of them.

The 9:30 AM traffic was slow, so there wasn't much action at the apple cart. We sat there for a few minutes watching the traffic go by. It was a really nice fall day, about 70 degrees, with sunshine and bright fall colors everywhere--a great change from the previous day. I was sitting there thinking how close we were to the finish, how happy I was to complete the ride and how much fun it really had been. I was thinking about all of the funny things that had happened along the road, kind of laughing to myself in a little bit of a daze, just staring off after the cars, when the owner of the apple cart made a comment about my riding attire and saddle.

"You don't look like any rider from around here," he said.

"Now why is that?" I asked.

"All these riders from around here ride in English saddles on big brown and black horses and look like they just came out of a magazine for some clothing and saddle company. It's disgusting. Now you look like you've put some miles on that saddle, and the way you're dressed it looks like you're prepared to go a few miles more."

I took a real hard look at myself. I had on Nike 990 running shoes, with tattered shoe laces, and small burrs in the laces from probably as far back as Texas. I had two pairs of running tights on, white over black. I had holes in the white ones so you could see the black tights coming through behind the knees and in the crotch. I had on white ankle socks and a purple bandanna around my wrist and another around my neck. I was wearing a shirt and had a sweatshirt tied to the saddle. The shirt was a Save the Rainforest T-shirt, primarily white with an illustration in color of the Rainforest on the front and back. The shirt was clean but had grass stains and grease marks on it that even Tide could not get out. My sweatshirt was black and it was tied with a piece of leather to the saddle. The sweatshirt hung down the side of the saddle dragging one arm against Sea Ruler's front right leg. I made quite a fashion statement!

Now I took a look at Sea Ruler, who had sweat stains coming down all four legs to his ankles. A little dirtier than usual, because he must have rolled last night. We only brushed him up in the morning under the belly and on his back where we put the saddle. That kept those areas clean and free of abrasions, but the rest of the horse looked pretty grimy, especially when the sweat mixed with the dirt from the roll the night before. It was hard to get all the spots off each morning in the dark, and we didn't find out how dirty he was until the next day after I'd already put in 5-7 miles in the dark. I had been riding in some tall weeds this morning and obviously picked up some big burrs which were tangled in his mane and tail. We were a bedraggled pair and, as the man said, looked as though we had put on the miles.

I had just finished my bruised apple and Ruler was nudging me for another. So I gave him the core, which I usually eat, seeds and all--good roughage. I was still hungry and the man said, "You want a really good apple?" I said, "Sure, but so does my horse." "Can you afford it?" He went rummaging around in the back and brought out two of the largest apples I had ever seen. They were as big as my hand and I had to cut them in half for Ruler to even get a bite into his half.

We sat there talking for a while longer. I knew the inevitable question was going to come up. Finally he asked me,"You aren't from around here, are you?"

"No, we're not. We're from Arizona."

He laughed and said in a sarcastic sort of way, "Looks like you rode from there, too."

I turned to him very slowly and, in a very serious and deliberate manner, said, "We did; we rode the whole way from Arizona and we just got here today."

He stopped laughing to see what else I was going to say. I waited about five seconds--seemed like an eternity--and then laughed and said "No, I'm just kidding. You'd have to be crazy to ride a horse that far."

He laughed with me in agreement and said, "You're right, damned straight, you'd have to be plumb loco to ride a horse that far. I thought you were serious."

I said, "No, I was just kidding. I'm not that crazy," and turned to tighten up the cinch on the saddle.

"You want another apple?"

"No, I've got to get going."

"Stop in any time for an apple."

"I'll do that; see ya later," I said and rode on.

Ten days later I drove by that same apple cart on my way back west in a Hertz rental car. I stopped to get an apple. As I got out of the car and walked up to the apple cart, the same guy walked up from the side of the stand. I looked into his eyes to see some glint of recognition. There was none. He didn't recognize me at all.

"What kind of apples are you looking for?" he asked.

"I'm looking for an apple for my horse."

It took him about five seconds and then a big ol' smile lit up his face from ear to ear. He said, "I didn't recognize you dressed in a nice jacket and not on a horse."

I said, "Yeah. I still want an apple, though, and I have money to pay now."

"It's on the house," he said and went in the back and brought out the big apples again.

"How do you ever make any money at this if you give all these apples away to people that ride by on horses?" I asked him.

"I don't see that many people ride by that I would give an apple to, and, besides, I don't need the money. I just do this for fun. Where's your horse?"

I told him he was at a farm in Poolsville, Maryland, resting.

"You rode him all the way to Poolsville?"

"No," I responded, "we trailered him up there and I'm heading back to Arizona."

"I thought so," he said. "That's a long ride; must be 75 miles from here. I thought you might be riding that horse back to Arizona."

I laughed and said to him, "No, you would have to be pretty crazy to ride that far."

He laughed and said, "You're right, damned straight, you'd have to be crazy," and quietly added, "It'd sure be fun though. Have a good trip."

October 12, 1989. Disaster struck and our truck was out for the full eight count. We were just preparing to ride the stretch to the Potomac river and across the Memorial Bridge into D.C. that day. But the truck's catalytic converter went out. To ride the horse 2900 miles we had put 9000 miles on that truck, trailering back and forth, and it still had to go 2500 miles back to Tucson.

I spent the whole day in the Ford truck shop waiting for the truck to be repaired. They completed the work at 5:00 PM, under warranty, thanks to the Jim Click dealership in Tucson, who donated the vehicle. And we were on our way.

I drove back out to pick up Brad and Joyce and found Bob and Bea there with the media. Bill Pollard, owner of the house we broke down in front of, was, interestingly enough, a previous owner of Al-Marah horses, and he knew of Mrs. Tankersley and the ranch. He gave Joyce and Brad some lunch and called the media people, who arrived there about the same time I did. We did a few interviews and hooked back up and drove on to our last base camp in Maryland. We would return the following day to complete our ride in to the Potomac. Our finish on the 14th would have to be postponed one day. At the time it was very frustrating, but, in looking back, it really worked out well. This allowed us to ride through D.C. on a Saturday rather than on a busy Friday with traffic, and it tied in better with our last fund-raiser.

On October 13, 1989, I rode the 31-mile stretch just west of the Potomac, rode across the Potomac and into what I consider D.C. to the Lincoln Memorial. Bumper-to-bumper traffic from 6:00 AM to 9:00 AM. Two newspapers caught up with us along the route, the Faquier DEMOCRAT in Warrenton, Virginia, and the LOUDOUN TIMES-MIRROR in Leesburg, Virginia.

Riding through bumper-to-bumper traffic, passing out brochures like a modern day Johnny Appleseed, does attract attention. I was, in all honesty, making better time than the cars I was riding past. It is interesting that I recall this same scenario on the west coast in L.A. How appropriate--the worse environmental conditions at the start and at the finish. Seems as though it has a lot to do with people. Maybe

Sea Ruler and Lucian 50 miles east of Washington, D.C.
Courtesy of Victoria Bellerose by permission of <u>Loudoun Times Mirror</u>

we could create an algebraic equation something like this: the greater the number of people in a given area, the greater the environmental impact. Not always true, but in most cases the equation would hold.

This was Friday, and we finished the first part of our ride at the Lincoln Memorial. Brad had March Along with him so we unsaddled Sea Ruler and loaded him up and drove through D.C., past the White House and on up Pennsylvania Avenue to a point just east of D. C. city limits.We unloaded March Along and saddled up, and I continued riding another 10 miles toward Chesapeake Beach.

The little leapfrog which we had learned back in Ohio left us with six miles to ride in the D.C. area from the Lincoln Memorial to the White House, and then past the Capitol and east out Pennsylvania Avenue. We also left the last four miles to the beach. A total of ten miles left to go. We did this so we could ride the D.C. piece on Saturday, early in the morning, and be available to attend a fund-raiser in the evening. We would catch the last four miles on Sunday late in the morning, ride into Chesapeake Beach, and finish at about 1:00 PM.

On Saturday, October 14, at about 7:00 AM, we were all set to trailer into D.C. for our ride through. We were scheduled to meet some press people in front of the White House at 10:00 AM, so we had some time to do a dry run through. We drove the route with Brad so he would know where to meet us at each press stop along the way. We wanted the trailer and the banner in as many pictures as possible. There were tourists, joggers, and demonstrators everywhere. We had several photographers and a TV station catch up with us at the White House, around which I rode, and then on up to the Capitol where we stopped for some photographs.

We soon found out that we were not allowed on the lawn, and, furthermore, since we did not have a permit for that specific jurisdiction in D.C., they threatened to confiscate March Along and arrest us. The encounter went something like this:

A big security officer and a little security officer walked up to us as I was trying to position March Along for the Equus Photographer. You know, in those TV shows like Candid Camera, the photographer keeps telling the subject to back up a little more and then a little more, until finally the subject backs right off a cliff or falls over a chair or some other obstacle. Well our obstacle was that duo of security officers.

The photographer had his face in the camera and kept asking me to back this way and that way. Little did I know that two officers had come down from the White House to see what we were doing, riding around the White House lawn. They positioned themselves right behind March and didn't say anything to me or the photographer for a minute or two. I didn't even know they were standing behind me, so I kept backing and backing until I heard a very loud "Umm, ummm, excuse me."

I wheeled March Along around to find ourselves face-to-face with the officer duo. I noticed in the grass below that March Along's last step

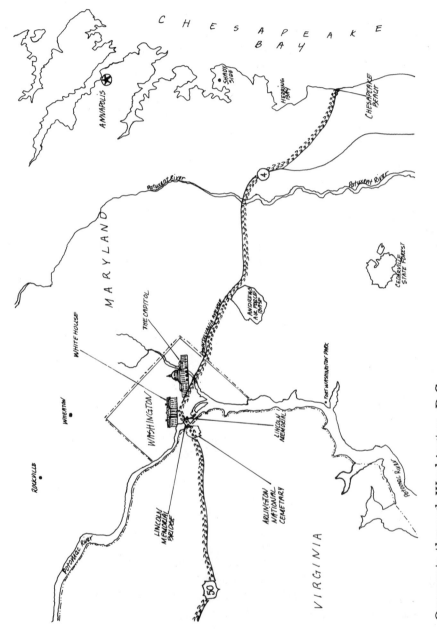

Our route through Washington, D.C.
Courtesy of Molly Zehr Palmer

March Along and Lucian in Washington, D.C. at the Capital.
Courtesy of Tim Davis, Equus Magazine

backward was inches from the duo. March Along was now nuzzling the little officer who was doing everything he could to defend himself and remain professional. I could tell he wanted to let his guard down, but he couldn't because the other officer was still drilling me with questions. March Along, however, was persistent and continued in his search for a carrot or some other hand-out and both officers finally gave in to his persistent head butts and began petting him. I pleaded innocence, that we were not well informed by police earlier. Other than this and the media we had with us, no one really paid much attention. That was not unusual, since, that same day on the lawn in front of the Capitol, four different demonstrations were going on. In a sense, we were number five, and to all of us it was a very big deal. But media-wise we got only token coverage. Still, were very happy with the results.

That evening we had a fund raiser in Catlett, Virginia, with Terry Dudis. A high school friend of mine from Athens, Ohio, Terry read about the ride in the Equus Magazine and became an enlistee in our effort. She and Marie Ridder, a member of our board of directors, offered to have a get-together and celebration for the finish. This event was to occur on the last day of the ride, but because of the truck failure and our one-day delay, this celebration was one day early. I was not complaining--we had a good turn-out and good media coverage. It was a fitting public finale.

We gave some awards out to the team members, Brad and Joyce and Bob and Bea, had some cold drinks and we had a very relaxed time. Terry had a one-acre grass paddock where the horses had a chance to stretch their legs. This was the first time in four months that they were not confined, and they spent at least a half-hour running, kicking and cavorting in the pen while all of the people at that party stood and watched in awe. It was a real show. They were running so fast that Sea Ruler threw his Easy Boots. I planned to ride him the last four miles into the beach the next morning, so we put them back on. I'm glad the finish was the next day because it gave me a chance to complete the ride in a more private way with the people who really helped me make this happen.

Sunday, October 15, 1989: We awakened at about 8:00 AM. We only had to trailer about 10 miles and ride four. No big deal. A piece of cake. Everyone was pretty calm and quiet; seemed like a pretty normal day on the ride. We got the horses loaded and drove to the drop-off point. Brad and I rode in the truck with the horses, and everyone else went on to the beach. If I would trot most of the way, it would only be a one-hour ride. Brad and I were driving down this road, not saying a word. It was weird--it would be the last time that we would drive together like this--and neither of us could say anything. I wanted to say so many things, like "Thanks for sticking it out; you made it happen; I learned a lot from you," and on and on. But nothing came out.

We had done this same drive so many times over these last five months. We were so different and, at the same time, so similar. I broke the ice by saying--what else--"Well, this is it."

Brad replied, "Sure is. It's been a long road."

I replied "Yeah, that's for sure," and we both laughed.

That was it. That pretty much sums it.

Now we had agreed in camp to take a shortcut to the drop-off point. This shortcut was not well marked, and, believe it or not, we got lost. On the last day, four miles from the beach, we could not find the drop-off point that I had marked the day before.

We back-tracked and came down the road on a more familiar route and quickly found it. About a 30-minute delay; we were a little ahead of schedule, so no big deal. Bob was waiting for us at the drop-off point, and, when we finally pulled up, he found Brad and me, as usual, arguing over whose fault it was. I was arguing and laughing at the same time and I think Brad was as well. Even so, he was putting up a good fight. I just remember saying, "I can't believe it. After all these days we get lost on the last day."

I'm going to win this last argument, though, because I have the last say, and the only way Brad can get in the last word is to write his own book. Here it is, the last word: Brad missed the second turn coming out of camp. There, I did it. Maybe, and that is a big maybe, I might not have seen the turn.

Now we were at the finish. We had been riding for 150 days. We'd gone 2963 miles. What do I say? It was an intense challenge that required every bit of mental and physical energy I could muster every minute of every day. I wanted it that way. I wanted to feel the sun and the wind and the heat and the cold. I wanted to be on the emotional and physical edge. I asked for that challenge. I kept the tension level up, and by and through my example, I asked the other team members to maintain a high level of concentration for the duration of the event. We did this ride under very difficult physical conditions over a very long period of time, and we stretched every aspect of the ride to the limit. We stretched ourselves both physically and mentally; we stretched our horses, our equipment, the media, those who helped; we pushed very hard, and at the prospect of finishing I was, in a word, relieved. We made it, we beat the odds, we persevered within ourselves and within each other and we gained the cooperation of so many.

I wrote in my journal in Missouri: "I feel a growing burden to finish and it emanates from those who've helped and we are now riding for these people. They are the real reason I keep riding."

The rainforest is a very important issue; it has long-range global implications and is, I firmly believe, the most pressing environmental problem facing us today. But what is most important is how people relate to this crisis and how effective we are at convincing people that this is, in fact, very important. I continue to believe, as I did when I began this ride,that the best way to convince someone you are sincere and care is through your example. We cared enough about this issue

Lucian and Sea Ruler going over the Sea Wall, Chesapeake Beach.
Courtesy of Char Magaro

to take on this challenge and ultimately finish. That to me is the example I want to leave with you.

As we rode onto the beach, people were popping champagne corks everywhere, the sun was shining and the sky was very blue. There were some clouds hanging on the horizon and I remember thinking to myself that the sun rises here. I've been riding into these sunrises for almost half a year now, and this is where it ends.

Brad was holding March Along, and Sea Ruler must have known something was up--people were hollering and yelling congratulations--because he had his tail up, which he never did before, and his ears forward. He saw that big ol' body of water and must have said: "No way am I going in there." I thought of Sweet William's first step into the ocean on the west coast 150 days ago. It seemed like so very long ago. At this point in the bay there are no real open areas--it is all private property, built up with condos and residential housing. So to get to the beach we had to get the permission of a condo owner to ride on through the property and over a small rock retaining wall; then we were in the water. All of the condo people were there to wave us on through. I smiled.

Someone poured champagne on me and Sea Ruler, and Bea gave me a big kiss. Then we all got together and did some video and some final interviews. I took some pictures with my Aunt Katie and Uncle John, and Uncle Chuck and cousin Lenny, who had come in from Alexandria to see the finish. My father drove in from Ohio, and it was great to have all of them there. Everyone was in very good spirits.

Brad and I rode both horses into the water and up and down the beach for quite a while; we gave Char and Ona a ride. They came down from Harrisburg for the finish. Then Brad and I shook hands, and that to me was significant. Brad was an integral part of this ride and our success. He managed those horses as no man I know could have, constantly playing the odds, the trade-offs between injury, distance and fatigue. Like a conductor of an orchestra who knows just when to use the right instrument, he played those horses.

Bob and Bea, Joyce and Brad, and the horses and I got a chance to thank each other on video. Bob and I talked for a emotional minute and then drank some more champagne. I took off the cowboy boots I was wearing when I rode into the water, and I've never worn them since.

At the finish I felt relief; I felt as if a big burden had, in one sense, been lifted from my shoulders and then replaced with a even heavier burden. As I was riding the last mile into the beach I said to myself, "I can't let all this end here. I need to build on this and the discovery I made back in Texas, that you truly never really fulfill your commitment to making this a better place in which to live." This commitment became my new burden. I remember actually thinking about that as we were riding into the water. I didn't mind at all. Once again, if you can believe this, I was a little preoccupied with these thoughts. I was thinking as we rode into the water about how we could keep this alive. I wasn't really all there, and the significance of that moment, as so often happens, didn't really sink in 'til months later.

The finish, Lucian and Sea Ruler in Chesapeake Bay.
Courtesy of Char Magaro

The finish, the Team at Chesapeake Beach in Chesapeake Bay.
Courtesy of Char Magaro

Perhaps an excerpt from a letter I wrote to one of our board members captures the essence of my feelings during the last moment of the ride: I feel it sums up my thoughts immediately after the event much better than I can now, one year later.

November 8, 1989

To A Board Member:
(An excerpt from a letter)

"Well we made it. One year to the month after first talking to you, 150 days on the road and 2963 miles. It has just now begun to set in. In looking back I am really happy to have had the opportunity to do the ride. It was not always apparent to me during the event that we were really accomplishing something of great significance.

The ride did not turn out to be the event that would shake the world and awaken the world to the cause. In almost a desperate way I wanted it to be that event and I tried very hard to meet all of the expectations and objectives early on. By the time we hit Texas it was apparent to me that it was not going to be the event that I wanted it to be and that if we were going to finish I would have to concentrate and focus all of our energy on the most important aspects. At that point the evolution of this event took its most significant turn. I began to focus on the people we met along the way and in a sincere way tried to convince them that the cause was important. I put a lot of energy into getting accurate press coverage on the issue. I also discovered that the desperation I felt came from my own feeling that this would be my last hurrah and that after completing this event I would have fulfilled my commitment to making this place a better world. When I discovered that this was not to be the case and that you really never fulfill that commitment I began to enjoy the event a lot more and was less desperate. That discovery did not come a moment too soon. It was still a very difficult event both physically and mentally for all of us, my weight dropped to at one point 147 lbs and Brad said he lost at least 20 lbs. But I was confident in the fact that I knew if we could continue to focus we would make it. . . . "

Sincerely,

Lucian

9

OUR FUTURE ENVIRONMENT:
THE ENVIRONMENTAL RIDDLE

What do we know for sure? We know that the future will be different from today. We know this because today is already different from yesterday. We can count on this. Change is occurring rapidly, and technology is the driving force behind this. Technology is a double-edged sword and what we are able to quickly change with positive results can also be altered in an ecologically negative manner as well. The rapid change brought about by technology, the speed at which it is occurring and the resulting impact--this is our dilemma.

"But in the last few generations mankind's propensity to change his environment has itself been transformed, as symbolized by the contrasts between the waterboat and the radar-equipped factory ship, the water wheel and the nuclear power plant, or the country road and the interstate highway. The power to use and adapt has become the power to destroy abruptly."[1]

The resulting impact can be seen, for example, in a comparison between the impact that a local mill on a small river or stream in the early 1900's had on the ecosystem in contrast with the global or regional impact large hydroelectric dam projects now have on Brazil or even on the western United States just 60 years later.

We know for certain that there has not been a day in the last four and a half billion years that the earth has not undergone change. We also know that humans, unlike other organisms, have consciously been able to alter and modify the environment. Our inclination to do so has grown dramatically over the last century and, more specifically, within

[1]Robert Dorfman and Nancy Dorfman, "Economics of the Environment," W.W. Norton and Company, New York, N.Y., 1977.

127

the last two generations. Technology has given us this power. With it we can adapt and quickly modify the environment as we see fit. We are learning, however, that technology cuts both ways.

Physicist Albert Schweitzer once said, "As we acquire knowledge, things do not become comprehensible but more mysterious." Today, I often hear that we are the most educated and informed generation. Then why is it that we are not able to understand, acknowledge or accept the critically important connection we individuals have with the environmental tragedies we read about? To many, our natural world remains a mystery. We have become a complicated society, and when we refer to our quality of life we concern ourselves with education, the arts, the homeless, AIDS, cancer and a host of worries and wants.

In the near term, to cope with the various demands and concepts it will be necessary to make incremental changes--in essence, to plug the dike so that we can bring under control quickly the most threatening activities. To do this will require patience, compromise, cooperation and sacrifice. We have a host of wants and needs in society today that impose upon us. For our near future, we need to find a balance. To do this, we should quickly identify those activities that represent the biggest threat, put them in order of priority, and then throw the majority of our resources, technology, money, and expertise at them now. On less critical issues, seek an accommodation and give a little to get a little. I would suggest that the immediate problems would include the rainforest issue, energy, consumption, the ozone problem and the oceans. That would be my immediate hit list.

Our challenge now is three-fold. First, we must, as individuals, bring that extremely important interrelationship--the balance of nature--back into focus. We must understand that we play the most important role.

Real knowledge is our most powerful tool. If we can help individuals come to environmentally sound conclusions on their own, we will have made important progress. The logic and intuition individuals employ in reaching the conclusion will motivate them to act.

Second, we must focus on the pending marriage between the economy and the environment. They need to be one and the same; until death do they part.

In the last 35 years, our society has had the benefit of unprecedented growth and prosperity. It is now apparent that our rise in economic well-being has brought on a host of social and economic problems. We can no longer say that further growth will solve our problems. Quite the contrary--we can say, in fact, that society is suffering the consequences of a growing economy. We cannot say with certainty that all of our problems are the result of mismanagement, evil companies, greedy bureaucrats, uninformed politicians, and irresponsible special interest groups. Rather, they are a result of all of these factors.

The most important role we, as individuals play, is the role of consumers. If we make environmentally sound decisions in the market and cast our ballot for environmentally compatible products, the market will respond. In the United States we have 5 percent of the world's population and we consume 25 percent of the world's oil. We are a consuming, not a conserving society. We need to consume less and we need to recycle. If we simply do this, many of our environmental problems would be solved. So the biggest single contribution we, as individuals can make is in our role as consumers.

Finally, in our three-fold challenge we need resolve and commitment to preserve, conserve and restore the balance.

Preservation and conservation are two very different environmental terms. Preservation is a term that connotes protection from harm or damage. For example, preserving the Alaskan wilderness would require that people not be allowed to intervene. The area would remain authentic in years to come. Conservation, on the other hand, implies that it is acceptable for us to manage our resources in a sustainable manner. But what is an appropriate use of a resource to one person, may mean something entirely different to someone else. In our society the two terms are often contradictory. Simply put, we should preserve what we can when we can, conserve what we can't preserve and restore.

Our ecosystem is amazingly resilient. Given a chance, it will come back strong and vibrant, like the restored lakes we rode by in Ohio. Ecological restoration efforts are a more offensive approach in contrast with typical, more traditional defensive approach in either conservation or preservation. Restoration is a conscious attempt to compensate for our influence on the system. But we can undo influence only as we understand it. To correct the harm we impose on our natural system, it is necessary to understand the precise nature of that imposition. And this, in turn, presumes that we fully understand the system itself. By committing ourselves to restoration, this cycle of influence and compensation, we obligate ourselves to seek a more exact understanding of our influence on the environment. This emerging "new understanding" will then have a positive influence on our future relationship with nature and the decisions we make. With this in mind, it is very important that we aggressively embark on the road to restoration and discover many new and better alternatives.

PRESERVING, CONSERVING, AND RESTORING OUR ENVIRONMENT

Here I present some of my thoughts on how we can go about preserving, conserving and restoring our environment. Because they are all interlinked, working on one specific area, for example preserving the rainforests, will affect other areas.

For clarity, I have divided my concerns into the following areas: rainforests, ozone, energy and coal, Chesapeake Bay, and the environmental movement.

RAINFOREST

To understand the global impact of deforestation, we must first understand the basic biology of the rainforest and the causes of deforestation. After this we can discuss some of the factors which cause the rainforest to influence global climate and weather patterns.

Rainforests cover less than 7 percent of the globe. They are predominantly found in a wet or moist band circling the globe along the equator. Tropical rainforests are the richest, oldest, most productive and genetically diverse ecosystems in the world. Between 40 and 50 percent of all living organisms (plants and animals) on this planet live in the rainforest.

What characterizes a rainforest? Temperature and rainfall. The equatorial rainforests, which represent about two-thirds of the world's rainforests, receive more than 250 inches of rain per year. The average temperature is 80 degrees Fahrenheit, with no seasonal fluctuation in temperature during the year.

The second main group of tropical rainforests receive less rainfall-- 40-160 inches per year--and has distinct wet and dry seasons. These seasonal rainforests are not as genetically diverse as the equatorial rainforests.

In years past, the rainforests covered over 14 percent of the earth's surface. Now they cover less than half of this. Most of the destruction has resulted from human intervention in the last 200 years, and more specifically since 1950. Of the remaining rainforests, almost 60 percent are located in Latin America.

Most people in developed countries are so far removed from nature they are unable or unwilling to perceive the relevance or relationship of rainforest organisms to their daily life. They do not know that many products they use come directly or indirectly from tropical rainforests. Some of the more common products are rubber, teak, mahogany, pesticides, medicinally useful drugs like quinine, cocaine, diosgenin and many active anti-cancer compounds. Some food items include cashew nuts, avocado, mango, cocoa, coffee, and spices like vanilla and nutmeg.

We know that 25 percent of all prescription drugs marketed in the United States contain one or more plant compounds. We can assume that many new drugs are awaiting discovery in the rainforest, yet fewer than 1 percent of tropical species have been examined for their possible use to mankind. As deforestation continues, millions of yet undocumented and documented species of plants and animals die. There are literally thousands, if not millions, of yet-to-be discovered species which could one day yield vital or economically valuable products.

Deforestation means the removal of large tracts of tropical forest for

RAIN FORESTS

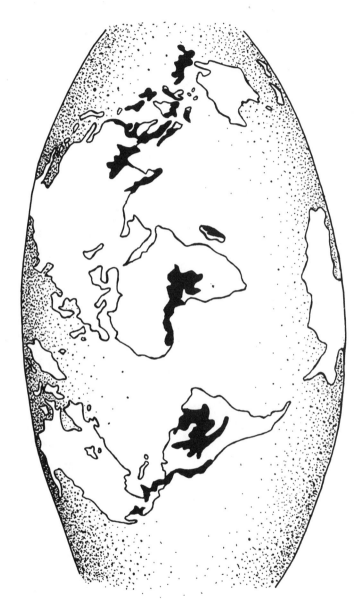

The earths tropical rainforests wrap around the world in a band that dominates areas in Central and South America as well as parts of Africa and Indonesia.

Courtesy of Rosemary Renteria and Angie Wood

agricultural, urban, or industrial use. A primary or virgin forest is one that has been undisturbed for centuries. If it has not been disturbed, it is often called a climax forest, which means it is no longer going through stages of development. It is at this mature stage that the rainforest is the most diverse and complex. Once primary forests are disturbed in any manner, they are no longer in equilibrium and they are classified as secondary forests. Human intervention is usually the cause.

Forest conservation implies that our use of the forest comes with a degree of preservation. Wise use of the forest involves some type of trade-off between preservation and development. The gene pool and genetic diversity refers to the quantity and variety of the individual organisms, populations, or species in the forest. The gene pool is commonly referred to as a natural resource, available through the process of natural selection.

In some cases we can alter organisms through genetic engineering and selective breeding and change the organisms to meet some human requirement. We often see the gene pool as a renewable resource and in most cases it is. In the rainforest, however, it can quickly become a non-renewable resource as species become extinct through loss of habitat. When a species becomes extinct, we lose that gene code forever. Tropical rainforests serve as a bank of genes which can, and currently do, provide products of economic and medicinal importance to people in both developing and developed countries.

One example of why a gene bank is very important can be seen in the Corn Blight of 1968. In the summer of that year, in isolated cases farmers noticed a mysterious disease on their corn plants. This was the first sign of a very dangerous fungus that reproduced rapidly in the warm moist weather of 1970. Under these conditions, the disease spread across the Southeast, toward the United States cornbelt. It left the cornfields in shambles. It was called the Southern Corn Leaf Blight. In four months it spread from Georgia into Oklahoma. It spread so quickly because the United States corn crop was genetically uniform, so what affected one plant affected them all. For this reason a diverse gene pool is very important.

Rainforests are being destroyed or severely degraded at a rate of 100 acres per minute--every minute of the day, every day of the week and every week of the year. The United States National Academy of Sciences reports that an area the size of England, Scotland and Wales (50 million acres) is lost each year. At this rate, we will lose all of the world's remaining rainforests by the year 2050, just sixty years from now.

What are the causes of this devastation? The four primary causes are 1) commercial logging, 2) fuelwood gathering, 3) cattle ranching, and 4) small scale forest farming and population pressure. The causes are complicated since they are at the same time political, psychological and economical. Many people claim that the rainforests must be developed and conquered to help the poor and landless. Or in some cases, settlement of civilians by the government is meant to secure national borders by establishing a presence in the frontier region. In Panama, for example, the government can rally support around this policy and establish a new frontier where the poor can find land and start fresh. Thus, psychological pressures directly or indirectly influence various public officials and governments as they establish guidelines for the development of what they consider to be a resource.

Some tropical forests are increasingly exploited because more people want more wood. Consumption of wood is expected to increase by 135 percent during the last years of this century. Of the total, one-third of the wood will be used as fuel in developing countries. Over 50 percent will be used in developed countries, where there has been a rapidly growing demand for hardwood. These hardwood products are used in the construction industry as plywood, veneer and particle board.

The largest single consumer of tropical hardwood is Japan, which imports almost four-fifths of its wood from tropical forests. Many developed countries are self-sufficient in producing pulp for their various paper products. Japan, on the other hand, imports over half of what it needs, and the requirements are expected to increase. The United States is the second largest consumer of tropical wood. Into the early 1980's, southeast Asia was the primary source of most tropical hardwood. As a result, the forests in this area are nearly depleted and the timber industry is now turning toward Latin America to meet the growing demand.

In Brazil, cattle ranching was the largest contributor to deforestation. Until the 70's, the government sponsored a program that promoted colonization. The government gave incentives to ranchers to exploit the rainforest and develop either farming or ranching interests. A large percentage of the clearing that took place was a result of various government incentives. But cattle ranching proved to be inefficient. In many countries, meat production on a pound per acre basis is ten times what ranchers in Brazil will receive. Once the rainforest is cleared, the pasture has a life expectancy of less than eight years. The land is laid to waste and the rancher will then need to move on. The degradation caused by long-term ranching seems to be one of the biggest problems facing Latin America now.

American consumers are a driving force behind the spread of ranches in the Latin American rainforest. Beef from Latin America is less expensive than our homegrown beef. Most of this Latin American beef goes to fastfood restaurants or products such as hot dogs and hamburgers. Beef that comes in from Central America is grass-fed and too lean for the typical American's taste. That suits the fast food industry well, for this beef is simply combined with United States beef and the combined product is then sold as "American" grade meat. Conservationists have in the past promoted a boycott of the fast food industry, and many restaurants now swear that they no longer use

Latin American beef. This is very hard to disprove, however. Combination meat products are difficult to trace primarily because, once imported beef is inspected, it is allowed to enter the United States market without any requirement indicating its country of origin.

Another factor contributing to deforestation is world population, which is growing at an ever-increasing rate. The largest percentage of this growth is taking place in developing countries in the rainforest region. Small scale forest (subsistence) farming, the search for fuel, and government programs to provide the landless poor with an opportunity to own property within the rainforest will, in the years to come, represent the largest threat to this ecosystem.

Most attempts to convert rainforests into farmland have failed. Farming, like ranching, will upset the delicate natural balance of the rainforest ecosystem and eventually, probably within six to eight years, leave the land so depleted that it will not be able to sustain crops or even pasture. In the rainforest, the nutrients reside in the biomass, rather than the soil. The biomass is the total weight of all of the organisms--plant and animal--in an area. The rainforest is so efficient and utilizes all of the nutrients so quickly, that it is always in a process of transformation. Therefore very few nutrients can be found in the rainforest soil. When a rainforest is burned, carbon is released and will for a short time act as a nutrient or fertilizer, allowing crops to grow. As soon as this ash is used up, though, the soil becomes barren.

If the causes for the decline in rainforests are complicated, the role that rainforests serve in the global balance of nature is simple. As a gene bank, the rainforest directly and indirectly protects all of the plants and animals on the globe, including the human population. Studies have shown that the rainforest can produce natural products that, in value, far outweigh agricultural or ranching products. Studies have also shown that these products can be harvested and sold for a sustained period of time. The economic worth of these rainforests for purposes other than ranching and farming is important to note because most of the rainforest countries are saddled with huge debts which could be relieved through economic reforms promoting conservation and preservation.

If the present patterns continue until the middle of the next century, all or most of the world's remaining rainforest will be lost. When the trees are cleared away, little except scrub grass and weeds will grow in the poor soil. When plants and animals that used these trees for cover are exposed and die, the once-lush forest is replaced with a desert. This desert area tends to grow larger and creates a very dangerous spiral: with fewer trees, less vapor rises into the atmosphere, which causes less rainfall, that in turn destroys more rainforest, and on and on.

Preserving this belt of rainforest along the equator is probably the most important environmental stand that conservationists can make. The political implications of success here are as important as the biological consequences. If, through long-term sustainable development, environmentalists can influence the preservation of this fragile ecosystem, they will have won a battle of global significance. It will indicate world-wide cooperation on the environmental problems that face all of us. It will also ensure that the gene bank will stay intact and help support other ecosystems around the world.

What are some actions that individuals can take? Probably the easiest thing we can do is to plant trees. Every tree absorbs carbon and every tree helps. Do not eat fast food products that come from the rainforest countries. Perhaps we need labeling laws to specify the country of origin of all food products. Start an educational program at school for students and invite the local media to attend. Find people in your area who have made a contribution to saving the rainforests and have the media highlight these efforts. Avoid purchasing or using tropical wood products. Promote a local boycott of these products. Write the Rainforest Action Network for the "Tropical hardwoods Booklet". Write Friends of the Earth for the "Good Wood Guide," which tells you about wood you should avoid. Lobby your senate and congressional leaders to support policies that reduce debt in developing countries. These policies should tie debt reduction in developing countries to environmentally-appropriate land use and energy policy.

OZONE

We hear so much about the ozone depletion problem. What is ozone? What does ozone actually do in the Earth's atmosphere? How does ozone effect life on Earth? Atmospheric ozone is a gaseous substance made up of three oxygen atoms. Ozone is formed in the stratosphere as a result of the absorption of ultraviolet radiation by oxygen. Ultraviolet radiation causes the O_2 (molecular oxygen) to dissociate into O (atomic oxygen). Some of the atomic oxygen combines with molecular oxygen to form ozone. This is represented by the following formula: $O_2 + O = O_3$.

Ozone is an unstable gas. It will break down into oxygen by absorbing more ultraviolet radiation. Hense, ozone forms and reforms continuously in the atmosphere at a rate that varies according to the amount of ultraviolet radiation present. Most ultraviolet radiation from the sun is absorbed by the ozone layer in the stratosphere. Ozone reaches about 10 parts per million at altitudes of 25-30 km, while at sea level it is only .04 parts per million. Even though the 10 parts per million is only a trace amount in the stratosphere, it protects life on earth from excess ultraviolet radiation from the sun.

The important point to note is that this balance in nature of the formation and destruction of ozone is fairly constant. If we reduce the amount of ozone in the upper atmosphere that is available to react with the incoming ultraviolet radiation, we will reduce the atmosphere's ability to protect us. The sun's ultraviolet radiation is rather constant, but we have the ability to affect the amount of ozone that is available to react with the incoming ultraviolet radiation. If we deplete or destroy the ozone layer, we will be allowing more ultraviolet radiation to reach the Earth's surface.

Ozone is layered in relatively small concentrations. More than 90 percent of all ozone is located in the upper region of the stratosphere; the rest is in the lower atmosphere. In spite of the small amount of ozone in the atmosphere, all life forms are affected by its presence or absence. Without ozone, all life forms (in particular one-celled plants and animals which form the basis of all food chains) will suffer from an excess of ultraviolet radiation, and no doubt will cease to exist.

The dependence of life on this very small amount of ozone in the atmosphere has been known for some time. In the 1920's, scientists first determined preliminary concentrations of ozone and ultimately its importance in absorbing ultraviolet radiation. Only recently, however, have scientists discovered that small amounts of other substances, chloroflourocarbons (CFCs) in particular, affect the quantity of ozone in the atmosphere. This makes it very likely that human activity, by altering these other substances, can alter the amount of ozone. A relatively small decrease in ozone would be likely to produce a significant increase in skin cancer. It is likely that the current reduced levels are already causing damage.

While ozone in the upper atmosphere serves as a shield to protect life on Earth from the harmful effects of ultraviolet radiation, ozone in the lower atmosphere serves as a pollutant. Ozone is produced on the surface of the Earth when hydrocarbons from incomplete combustion in vehicle engines react with nitrogen oxides in the presence of sunlight. The accumulation of ozone, carbon dioxide and chloroflourcarbons in the lower atmosphere may cause global warming.

There is evidence that increases in ultraviolet radiation will have a negative impact on the human immune system, which may lead to a higher number of viruses and infections. Aquatic life forms are also extremely sensitive to increased levels of radiation. Micro-organisms in the water are the basis of many food chains, and so their importance cannot be overestimated. Micro-organism species provide the major source of protein world wide and in developing countries the percentage is even higher.

Larger organisms are less affected by an increase in ultraviolet radiation than are smaller organisms. In larger organisms the internal organs are not exposed to the ultraviolet radiation, smaller organisms have less tissue mass to absorb the radiation.

How do we protect our planet from a increase in ultraviolet radiation as a result of a decrease in ozone? The only way is to control the use of chemicals that deplete ozone. Luckily, this may be one of the easier problems to resolve.

How does ozone depletion occur ? CFCs (Chloroflourocarbons) are man-made chemicals that drift up into the atmosphere and ultimately collide with ozone in the stratosphere. CFCs react with radiation in the stratosphere, releasing chlorine atoms. These chlorine atoms are free to roam the stratosphere, reacting with ozone. Their appetite is tremendous--each chlorine atom has the capacity to breakdown thousands of ozone molecules. CFCs have a life expectancy of 100 years. That means that once we release them into the atmosphere, it will take more than 100 years for them to break down and go away.

Scientists are not positive of this theory as revealed in CLEAR, CLEANER, SAFER, GREENER. Gary Null states, "we do not know enough about upper-atmospheric science or the chemical reactions between ozone and chlorine to really predict with any degree of accuracy what we can expect from our continued loading of chlorine into the atmosphere." So actually the impact could be significantly greater.

It might take three to five years for the CFCs that we release today to reach the stratosphere where they begin to feed on ozone. This means that if we quit using and producing CFCs today, it would still take 105 years--until the year 2095--to clean the atmosphere of CFCs. Although we can expect CFC production to continue into the year 2000, we are beginning to cut back production, which is a positive step in the right direction.

A large percentage of the CFCs are produced by a small group of companies. They are now facing pressure from environmentalists to discontinue production and find alternatives. It is working. In 1989, a group of European nations, the United States and Canada agreed to ban the use of CFCs by the year 2000. Later that year, a group of 81 countries agreed to enact the same deadline. On a more local level, many cities and states have begun to pass ozone protection bills as well. The result: Many large users, including Dupont, the world's largest producer, have agreed to phase out the production and use of CFCs in the 1990's. In the meantime, individuals as well must do their part and discontinue using CFC-related products. What are some of the things we can do to help?

Worldwide, spray cans are the largest source of CFC emissions. In the United States most companies are no longer producing them, but be aware and do not use them.

CFC is found in car air conditioners and home refrigerators. Check the car air conditioner for leaks. When you do this, take it to a station that has a Freon reclaiming unit. This way they can reclaim the Freon and recycle it. The Environmental Protection Agency says that automobile air conditioners are the single largest user of CFC's in the country. Home refrigerators are made with CFC coolant in them. Make sure the door seals do not leak and they are running properly. If you are going to throw away a refrigerator, make sure you drain the coolant first. Call a professional to do this.

When you go shopping, do not buy products that are packaged in polystyrene. CFCs are used to produce this material and will eventually leak back into the atmosphere. Eggs come in both cardboard egg boxes and polystyrene. Pick the eggs that come in cardboard egg cartons. Do not buy foam plates and styrofoam cups. If you need to buy throw-away products, buy paper plates and cups. If you can avoid buying them entirely, it is even better.

Check your fire extinguisher at home. Read the label and make sure it does not use a chemical called Halon.

One of the best ways to conserve energy and help the environment is to insulate your home. This keeps the house warmer in winter and cooler in the summer. Make sure you buy something other than rigid foam insulation. It has CFCs which will eventually get into the atmosphere. Use some other type and check the label to ensure that it is the correct value for the living space you are insulating. This value is the insulation's ability to insulate from heat and cold, which saves energy.

The above are things you can do as a consumer. As a citizen you can write a letter to your local Congressman or Senator. You can do this together with some friends. Tell your local political leaders that you would like to see them vote for laws that will immediately outlaw CFC production and usage at the local level. Ask your local political leaders to speak about their efforts to help stop this problem. Most of them will be willing to speak on the issues.

ENERGY

I remember reading in various magazines in the late 70's that nuclear energy would fill the energy gap and that within 30 years the majority of our energy would come from nuclear plants. The articles offhandedly said that nuclear energy would indefinitely postpone many of our environmental problems. After the Three Mile Island and Chernobyl accidents, the relatively high cost, and perception of danger have combined to put nuclear energy on the backburner, at least for now. Once again, consumers want less expensive energy. Currently coal is the least expensive, so we use it. We will continue to use it until it runs out or becomes more expensive; however, it is only inexpensive if you ignore acid rain, pollution, and new regulations.

At this point in this century, our energy prices at the pump and at home are subsidized--we consumers are not paying the true price. The cost of the energy we use is truly much higher. The market price does not accurately reflect the true cost to future generations; nor does it reflect the higher cost for new, yet-undeveloped technology. Until we take into account the present environmental cost and future impact, we will continue to consume subsidized energy. We will begin to look for alternatives and start conserving only when we begin to pay the true price. Much as we did in 1973 with OPEC and in the late 70's with nuclear energy, we must begin now to pay the real price as consumers and thereby promote alternatives and interim conservation.

In the book, 50 SIMPLE THINGS YOU CAN DO TO SAVE THE EARTH, it is argued that conservation does not mean "freezing in the dark," as Ronald Reagan once said. They propose some simple, cost-effective measures that require little change in life-style. William Chandler in "The State of the World--1987," says that the price-induced energy conservation response in the West since 1973 is the most significant conservation achievement of our time. We made very important strides since then, but only in response to a situation that was of immediate concern and financial impact to us all. My concern, once again, is that in 1973 we were responding to a financial crisis and we performed admirably. Until recently we have had no financial crisis to pressure us as consumers to demand change. Why? Because we have not been paying the true price. But we are again faced with a depressed economy facilitated by the 1990 Gulf Crisis. Hopefully, this time, we can gain a better perspective of the World's need to develop a program that will satisfy both economic demands and environmental needs.

We should study what France, Sweden and Japan are doing to conserve energy. But in making those comparisons we must be cautious. For example, in France nuclear fission is a primary source of energy. This source comes with its own set of trade-offs. Gary Null in his book, CLEARER, CLEANER, SAFER, GREENER lists the following myths associated with nuclear energy:

    1) Nuclear power is inexpensive
    2) Nuclear power is safe
    3) Nuclear power is clean

He goes on to state: "Nuclear technology is causing some of the most serious environmental contamination problems we now face. Unlike any of the other threats to our environment, nuclear power, no matter what we do, will remain here to haunt us for thousands of years." (Null, page 193).

One of the brightest lights at the end of the tunnel is alternative and renewable energy sources. Solar energy, wind, and geothermal energy represent three very appropriate sources of energy in the near future and beyond. It is very difficult to predict our energy needs 100 years hence or even 50 years from now. I am certain, however, that the pollution resulting from fossil fuels--oil, gas and coal--is now imposing a severe strain on our system. The sooner we begin to rely on alternative forms of energy, the sooner we can give this ecosystem a breather.

One alternative that has a lot of promise is solar energy. Solar energy has been around forever. Once a system of tapping this energy is in place, it is by far the most environmentally sound and least expensive system to operate. It is also passive and relatively maintenance-free. Why do we not move to this alternative right now? Cost. Typically the average homeowner can install a gas system for home heating for approximately $1250 while a comparable solar system will cost several thousand dollars. In other parts of the world, solar energy has a excellent track record and its success world-wide should warrant further research, investment, and experimentation.

When I rode through California, I was impressed with the windmill farms. Windmills used to be as common as the rural mailbox in the early part of this century. Then electricity, oil, and gas slowly took over the energy market. Nevertheless, the windmill farms I rode through in California generate a nice little chunk of the energy sold by utility companies in California. Wind power, however, has been plagued by the "it's an eyesore" mentality and various technical problems. With new technology and higher or more accurate oil and gas prices, wind could, in the future, with solar energy, serve as a very useful alternative.

Within the earth is heat that can be brought to the surface in the form of steam or hot water which can be converted to produce electricity. Many countries, including the United States, are tapping geothermal power. Japan and Iceland are leaders in the technology. Many say that it could, sometime in the 20th century, develop into a significant market. Once again, exploration, experimentation, and research are expensive. Discovering the full potential of geothermal power is simply a matter of "when"--when other sources become more expensive.

Hydroelectric power has been universally accepted worldwide. It is a relatively safe energy source and in its operational mode is more or less compatible with the environment. It does, however, do extensive damage to local habitat. In some areas, for example in the Brazilian rainforest, these projects have destroyed ecologically important habitat, caused flooding, and wiped out indigenous populations. Some dramatic and yet undefined environmental impacts of hydroelectric power are just now surfacing. Environmentalists are concerned with the change in water temperature and the potential catastrophic impact from a dam failure. The cost in some cases is prohibitive and the technology is still somewhat limited.

The very important relationship that we must understand is that, as consumers, we place a demand on the market that the market will attempt to meet. In some cases, we place a demand for ecologically inappropriate products. Our demand acts as the driving force behind what we consume and produce. We must quickly become aware of that relationship and learn to harness that potential. Consumers must demand that producers provide alternative products. What people in this country want and feel entitled to is having their cake and eating it at the same time. This is and will continue to be the underlying frustration of the ecology movement. The problems in America are linked to issues of too much rather than too little. The ecology movement must become more linked to economic problems and less to idealogy. I believe that ecological idealogy has in general ignored the context of economic development from which the problems of pollution have been generated. We must bring the two closer together.

For example, oil represents our largest source of energy in the United States, more than 42 percent. Cars and trucks require almost one half, or 45 percent, of the oil that we use. This level of usage is outrageously high in comparison to other countries. The American Petroleum Institute reports that transportation is where the nation needs to look first to cut its energy needs. Yet we still believe that it is less expensive to produce and consume than it is to conserve. This mentality has to change. We are consuming not only our share of energy, but that of other countries and that of generations yet to come.

COAL

Since the early 1970's, the idea that we can curb pollution by harnessing the market forces that drive the production and consumption of products has gained some credence. According to this theory, by focusing on the market we can indirectly penalize the producer and, further, we can force the producer to become more environmentally responsible. If we can allow the coal market to set a true and accurate price for coal, we should see a reduction in pollution. The rising cost of producing power with coal will force producers to employ alternatives. This idea has met with corporate and, in some cases, government approval. Some environmental groups, too, rally around the theory. Most environmental groups, however, see this as a viable concept in the long term but inadequate in the short term.

A more appropriate approach might be to develop a master plan that would identify the most cost-effective and environmentally appropriate uses of the different types of coal. This could be done on a regional basis according to the properties of the coal found in a particular area. With this approach, stack scrubbers would be required where needed (high-sulfur coal-producing regions), and, in the West, where we burn low-sulfur coal, they would not be required. The market would at least regionally influence the production and consumption of energy. In time, high-energy-consuming companies would opt to relocate to regions where utility charges are lower. This would drive those states with high-sulfur, high-cost energy to find alternative lower-cost sources. Over time this would reduce consumption and then lower prices as these new sources would be discovered. That is an idea. Whether it would work out that way, we can only speculate.

As I rode through Ohio and West Virginia, I encountered numerous streams that brought back memories of meandering hikes, fishing and swimming in this same area 20 years before. At that time, a popular swimming hole was Raccoon Creek. It is a small stream just 15 miles west of Athens, Ohio. At that time our swimming hole had a big rope tied to a railroad tressle. The railroad tressle crossed Raccoon Creek just before it went into The Moonville tunnel. If you had the courage, you could walk out onto the tressle and jump off or you could swing from the rope in a more exciting but shorter fall. The tressle was at least 50 feet high, and the rope which swung out over the stream was probably 20 feet high at its apex.

Three things I will always remember about that swimming hole: (1) Even from the tressle you could see the bottom of the creek. Before you took the big leap, you would always look first to see if any submerged debris might be floating your way just below the surface. (2) The water was yellow-green. And (3) there were no fish living in the stream and very little plant growth. My girlfriend Kim once said that she didn't want to swim in the stream because there might be fish that bite. I remember telling her that no fish lived in the stream so there was no need to worry.

In most of the other lakes and streams in Ohio at that time you could not see the bottom because of the proliferation of algae and other organisms that grew in the water. These were fertile, clean lakes and streams, and life grew as it should. But in Raccoon Creek, and some other area lakes and streams, the clarity of the water was not natural. Drain-off from strip mine pits or underground mines had seeped into the lake or stream and made the composition of the water uninhabitable for plant and animal life. In essence, these bodies of water were dead. Great for swimming, but dead.

In the past the method mining companies employed to bring coal out of the ground left areas stripped of vegetation and open to further degradation. The result--run-off into rivers and streams. Underground mining in this region left "gob piles" at the entrance of many mines. The gob piles left over from the mining operation are primarily low grade coal and shale. As with strip mining, these gob piles are a source of run-off into neighboring lakes and streams.

The problem stems from an impurity in coal called pyrite, or "fool's gold." Pyrite is an iron sulfide compound that is found in high concentrations in high-sulfur coal in this region. As pyrite breaks down to form sulfuric acid and iron sulfate, a yellow-orange residue commonly called "yellow boy" results. This residue seeps into the rivers and streams coating the bottom of the waterway and inhibiting growth of plant and animal life. Since that time, laws have been enacted that require companies that mine coal to seal off the underground mines and reclaim the land. This means that these companies are now required to bring the area back to a natural state. Some of these efforts have been successful and some have not. Many of these laws were retroactive.

When I was in Athens during my ride, I drove out to Raccoon Creek. It was still there, along with the Moonville Tunnel, but the tressle had been dismantled. My younger brother John said that kids no longer go to Raccoon Creek but instead have found other swimming holes. They now use a strip mine pit with the same symptoms as the stream: clear water and no natural plant and animal life. Raccoon Creek is still there and the symptoms persist. I took a look at the stream and found no evidence of improved water quality.

In another case, Lake Hope, a previously dead lake and my favorite swimming hole when I was younger, now offers swimming and boating and supports a very large population of bass and other game fish. By sealing the underground mines in the area and cleaning up and reclaiming many of the gob piles, the run-off of "yellow boy" and other residue into the lake has been reduced. The lake can now sustain normal plant and animal life. It is amazing how quickly that body of water rebounded. What was essentially a dead lake 20 years ago is now teeming with life. This is one situation where strict environmental policy worked. There is still a lot of work that needs to be done in older mining areas, and further legislation will be necessary to strictly regulate the industry. But progress is being made.

CHESAPEAKE BAY--A CASE STUDY

On May 15, 1990, we completed our ride to Chesapeake Beach on Chesapeake Bay, just east of Washington, D.C. How appropriate, I thought. From a scientific and ecological standpoint, Chesapeake Bay is without doubt the most studied and probably best-understood body of water in the United States.

Chesapeake Bay area is unique in two ways. First, it is a very unique ecosystem in and of itself, which generates a host of scientific opportunities. Second, the bay is an excellent case-study of environmental policy and planning. The bay borders several states. As a resource, it epitomizes the inability of various organizations, in the past, to coordinate efforts on a regional issue. It allows us to see how difficult it has been and still is to coordinate or even think on a global level. It should be viewed as an experiment in environmental trade-offs and as a study in "how we got here." It is a microcosm of a much larger world problem. Whatever we learn, in dealing with Chesapeake Bay as a regional problem, should be applied to problems in a more global sense.

Millions of dollars have been spent on studies examining the scientific aspects of this body of water and the results of abuses that go back as far as the mid 1700's. We have a huge scientific body of knowledge on a waterway that has been severely imposed upon. Until recently, little research has focused on the political and cultural influences on the bay. In the 1960's and 1970's, attempts were made to address the problems associated with comprehensive interstate planning. The first attempt was in 1933 with the formation of the Chesapeake Bay Authority. Not much came out of that conference, and little was done until 1964, when the Department of Chesapeake Bay Affairs was established and given the responsibility of developing a comprehensive plan for long-term management of the bay.

At the same time, another project was established to study water quality in the Chesapeake Bay-Susquehanna River Basin. However, the study never really got off the ground. Meanwhile, in 1966, the Chesapeake Bay Foundation was founded by a group of concerned citizens. This group now boasts 77,000 members and is a very strong influence in the area. In the same decade, conferences were held in Maryland and Virginia and plans were proposed for further studies. This activity at all levels, and in each state, led to the conclusion that this was a regional problem and must be addressed as such. It became clear that what the bay really needed was not a comprehensive plan that was all things to all people, but, instead, a "process" whereby the various states and competing interests could come to some compromise or decisions based on what impact this or that proposal might have on the Bay.

In the 1970's the big question was: "Is the bay dead?" This was a major turning point and to some extent reflects the general environmental attitude across the nation during that same time. Historically, scientists had jumped on the environmental wagon first and performed numerous studies and completed research on everything from fish kills to population density and its implications. After the results were published, a panic of sorts ensued. The studies raised public consciousness and showed that the ecological system was one interrelated cell. As this began to sink in, the public became more concerned with the overall health of the bay and less concerned with specific threats. This led to an important understanding, which brings us to a turning point--a decision point.

I see it as that point where we must accept certain facts, and those facts are that competing interests exist and will always exist. Progress in today's environmental arena should be seen as a search for environmental balance on a regional, and, similarly, on a global level. The Chesapeake Bay and its competing interests in oil and fishing is an example. Our first real step in the right direction will be our willingness to accept the fact that competing interests exist. Our second and bigger step in that same direction will be our first sincere step toward compromise. Only in this manner will we see true and real progress. The predominant concern now is for sustainability and the overall productivity of the global ecosystem. The decision to acknowledge or not is now upon us and a conscious search for adequate compromise is not far behind. It is not an either/or situation.

In 1983, Virginia, Maryland, Pennsylvania, Washington, D.C., and the federal government all agreed to establish a program to restore the Chesapeake Bay. That unprecedented cooperation was significant and represents what should and could occur on a global scale environmentally. It is probable that the resulting legislation and programs are helping. The Chesapeake Bay problem is still far from being resolved, but the progress that is occurring reflects the progress the environmen-

These students are spending a day on board a Chesapeake Bay Foundation vessel. Students take water samples and examine oysters which have been dredged from The Bay. The Chesapeake Bay Foundation takes over 35,000 students out on the bay each year.
Courtesy of Chesapeake Bay Foundation.

tal movement has been able to make thus far on a more global scale. The history behind cooperation and legislation in Chesapeake Bay parallels that of the environmental movement generally. Environmentally, as members of this ecosystem, we are at a juncture, poised to move ahead--or fall behind.

On the day the Los Angeles Lakers got their tails kicked by 34 points at the Garden (by Boston in game two of the "85" series), Pat Riley told his team a quote his father had once passed on to him: "Somewhere, someplace, sometime you're going to have to plant your feet, take a stand and kick some tail." Environmentally I believe that time is now. We are involved in a dangerous experiment and, with that in mind, we have to take a stand and gain control of our destiny. This will require that, as individuals and as a society, we must make certain sacrifices.

The technology already exists to clean up oil spills, develop alternative fuels, close the ozone hole, preserve the rainforests and stop or slow most environmental problems. It is important to realize that we do not need to go out and invent new technologies to fix all the problems. We already know many of the answers, and we know what we need to do to correct not all, but many, of the major problems. What we do not have is the resolve to focus on the problem.

As a thinking society we need to play out the trade-offs and make a concerted effort to set priorities, so that we can put the environmental issues at the top of the stack. Only when we do this can we channel our money, our technology, and our expertise into these problems and begin to see results. We need to do this as individuals first, through our consumption and the way we manage our own life-style. In parallel efforts, as the constituents of our elected leaders, we need to give these officials an environmental mandate. We must demand that our government approach the issue on a global level and coordinate with other countries to intervene on behalf of the environment.

This mandate is very important; the trade-offs are numerous. When making a decision, our government will need to know that we have the resolve and the commitment to go forth with the environmental issues. We may not need to invent anything: we already have many of the tools we need and also many of the answers. What we need to do is focus on the problem and get others to cooperate.

The most significant aspect of this ride, and of human nature in general, was the powerful emotional response that the environmental issue generated. This planet may be here for my generation and quite possibly the generation after mine, but will it be here for my grandchildren? This is the first time in the history of mankind that we are not entirely certain that in the near future our children will have a place to actually live. It has always been our desire to pass on to our children a better society and a better environment, be it the family farm, better education, or less disease and war. We are the first generation that won't be able to do this. Our children will instead be inheriting an over-used, hand-me-down that may be on its last legs and unable to support them and generations after.

What is so scary is that we might in this decade turn it all around, or we might not. If we don't, we have only ourselves to blame. We must rise to the occasion, take our lumps, and make whatever sacrifices are necessary to ensure that this planet survives and that we pass on to our children an ecosystem that can sustain generations in years to come. We must take control of our destiny. We all have an obligation to try and we all must try in our own way. I tried by riding a horse across the United States; Paul McCartney does it by having a concert; some do it by recycling; and others do it by simply reading this or other books and talking to others.

The director of Friends of the Earth, Michael Clark, said at our first Ride Across America news conference: "The most difficult thing to do is to explain to people the criticality of the problem without implying that it is too late and scaring them into doing nothing." I agree, and I add: "We show them the problem and we give them something to do." We give them the opportunity to become involved and we give them hope. Our ride was a way to attract attention to the issue and also to give many an opportunity to help. If we as individuals can provide an avenue of involvement, then this "Green Thing" will continue to grow. This "opportunity to get involved" will become more and more important as the movement grows and interest builds because people with no way to help become frustrated. The challenge for people like us who are already involved is to help others make that same commitment. If we can find ways to enlist others in our efforts, we can keep this ball rolling.

It is not too late. Far from it. This is a do or die decade, the decade that will set the stage in years to come. The ecosystem is amazingly resilient, and with help it can bounce back. The ecosystem's response to the changes we have imposed upon it is much slower than the rate at which we are imposing those changes. We need to let the ecosystem catch its breath so we can cross the finish line together.

We can see progress in many places. For instance, the recovery of lakes and rivers in strip mine areas across the United States; on a global level, Japan's recent commitment to improve economic conditions through loans and grants for environmental problems in debt-ridden countries; the phenomenal growth of membership in environmental groups; and Soviet leader Mikhail Gorbachev's call for an international Green Cross that would have international access to repair and prevent human damage to the earth. David Brower of the Earth Island Institute sensed the need as well and is now forming the "Green Circle." During a speech in 1989, he said that more than 80,000 people from all walks of life have responded thus far and are willing to commit a year in the next ten years to service in the organization.

The environmental havoc we have created in this finite planet may, with an unplanned twist of fate, be a blessing in disguise. Many would say that we are up against the wall environmentally. If so, it is quite possible that the desperation we feel may force us to join hands in a global effort to clean up the mess. This cooperation may reduce global tensions and allow us to focus on common ground, rather than economic and political differences.

Another positive step is the "Green Seal" of approval that will be coming out soon for consumer products. The seal will evaluate the environmental impact of specific consumer products as well as corporate performance. This is a solid, positive step toward consumption-preference purchasing. Those products with the "Green Seal" of approval will carry a strong message to the market place.

When the environmental movement began to emerge in the late 1960's, the members were willing to go to great lengths in an effort to challenge business policy. This approach seemed to justify itself as an attempt to bring attention to the new issue. The doomsday predictions and radical approach of the 60's, however, left a bad taste with the business community and the response was hard line. Over the next three decades, values, needs, and demands, combined with the ebb and flow of crises and attitudes on both sides, have brought on a mellowing, a sense of accommodation and maturing on both sides. In spite of this progress, controversy, conflict and misunderstandings continue to exist as both sides continue to voice strong opinions. But at least there is the awareness that dialogue and compromise are essential for any real progress. It is apparent now to both sides that we need a sustainable economy and a safe environment.

Three decades after its genesis, the environmental movement is legitimate, with renewed energy and interest. The business world now acknowledges the potential and actual impact this movement has on the market place. With more than 13 million members, more than 4,000 employees and a budget that annually exceeds a half billion dollars, the top 25 environmental groups are a force to be reckoned with. Nevertheless, the perception continues that the movement lacks an overall strategy and designated leadership, and among many of the members there still is quite a difference of opinion on both the overall direction and the approach to be taken toward environmental issues.

Often two or more organizations will defend the same issue. This overlap causes confusion and will often generate competition for funding and exposure. It also sends mixed signals to constituents and the business community. For example, the Rainforest Alliance, the Rainforest Action Network and the International Society of Tropical Forests, all focus primarily on the rainforest issue. In addition, several other groups receive funding to support this issue. Some of these groups may carry on work that differentiates them from one another, but from the outside looking in--donors, constituents, supporters and lay people in general--that difference is not always clear. And that confusion may stall or slow what could be astronomical growth in this movement.

Another problem is the ongoing tension within the movement between preservation and conservation (use). The movement has it's origin in the progressive conservation movement that began in the late 1800's. As economic demand for resources grew a difference of opinion began to emerge within the movement over our need to preserve resources (preservation) and our need to efficiently utilize our resources (conservation). This tension continues even today and will often influence the movements' ability to present a consensus to government and business on a specific topic.

In spite of the confusion, the movement is growing at a significant pace. In the near future, for economic as well as simplicity's sake, it would be advantageous for the members to distinguish themselves, so donations of money and time can be easily matched with clearly defined issues.

I see a shake-up of sorts in the movement, similar to the take-over frenzy on Wall Street in the 80's, fueled by a growing economy. The environmental arena is ripe; economies of scale will begin to play a more important role as these groups attempt to distinguish themselves from one another. The stronger organizations will merge with one another for purposes of efficiency and membership or to take advantage of the special abilities of one or the other. By and large, all of these mergers will be friendly and will help the movement to grow.

We can see this beginning to happen now with the most recent merger of the Environmental Policy Institute (EPI), Friends of the Earth, and the Oceanic Society. EPI had a good relationship with its donor base and strong support in Washington, D.C.; they were also running in the black and had a good management team. Friends of the Earth, on the other hand, needed a strong fund-raising arm. They brought their name and membership (over 40,000 members) to the merger table. This new organization now operates as Friends of the Earth, retaining the best of all three organizations. I see more of the same restructuring taking place over the next three to five years as the movement continues to grow. Competition within the movement is already very intense and will continue. As the movement grows, the clash between groups who are unable to distinguish themselves is inevitable. For further progress to be made, the movement will need to develop a common strategy, a framework within which to work toward common objectives, and a greater willingness to cooperate with one another and outside interests.

Recently, changes in the economic structure in Europe and other parts of the world have caused business interests to think on a more global scale. Technology has made this a very small planet, indeed, and has forced many in the business world to change their way of thinking. A decade ago it was commonly thought that resources, technology, labor, land, air and water were virtually infinite. The typical corporate horizon was short-term (10 years) and regional. This viewpoint was in conflict with the ecologist's long-term, global view of the world in which we live. However, for a number of economic and ecological reasons, that corporate view of the world is changing to a more finite and global approach. For the most part, business people and environmentalists now agree we need a sustainable economy and a safe place in which to live. For the first time, this agreement is more than just rhetoric, and that is a significant step in the right direction.

The market does not always reflect the true costs born by society from current environmental and economic decisions. But we will eventually pay the piper--if not now, then in the future. In the destruction of our rainforests, for example, countries and companies that harvest lumber from the rainforests are not paying the real cost for that lumber. They are not required to pay the cost that future generations will bear in cleaning up the environment, nor are they paying the cost of lost opportunities for pharmaceuticals that could be developed and losses in sustainable agricultural crops for the indigenous tribes. These are all costs that have not been included in the price we pay for that lumber.

Until we take into account all of these costs and make the consumers of rainforest products pay the true and higher prices, the devastation will continue. Governments must intervene and correct the market price to truly reflect the actual costs by charging a price for energy, rainforest, water and air. Until this happens, an important niche in our movement demands to be filled. The lag that often exists in the market's ability to truly reflect environmental costs is running up a future tab that is astronomical. This is a problem we need to confront now, and we must do this in conjunction with our other efforts. Some progress is being made here, but it is still not adequate.

The recent Economic Summit in Paris, in July, 1989, was termed the "Green Summit." For the first time, there was agreement among the countries that further economic progress is inextricably linked to world-wide environmental conditions. In developing countries, too, environmental awareness is beginning to surface. In Mexico, a country ridden with debt, economic woes, and an exploding population, a growing environmental movement within its borders has had some effect. Dozens of groups have sprung up across Mexico to protest a number of issues: increased oil drilling in the Baja, nuclear power, nuclear waste disposal, growing industrial waste resulting from the boom in "Maquilladora" plants along the border, and so on. These very influential groups have made headway in a country that is torn by political trade-offs. This is very encouraging news.

In other ways, individual consumers have an impact. We can make environmentally sound investment decisions. As shareholders in both large and small companies we have a voice, and one of the most important things we can do is require that our companies choose environmentally sound approaches to production and the business of doing business. Various money management firms have established socially responsible funds that guarantee our investments will be used

Rainforest before slash and burn in the state of Rondonia, Brazil.
Courtesy of Randall Gingrich

Slash and burn in the State of Rondonia, Brazil. Clearing the land for ranching and crops.
Courtesy of Randall Gingrich

in a socially responsible manner. These funds require that companies address the effects of their business on society and the environment.

The poet Wendell Berry once said: "How superficial and foolish we would be to think that we could correct what is wrong merely by tinkering with the institutional machinery. The changes that are required are fundamental changes in the way we live."

We know though that living implies that we consume. A result of this consumption is some level of waste. As society goes about the business of producing goods and services for the market, its activities are not 100 percent efficient. Production of goods and services and waste are not mutually exclusive of one another. One waste is a result of the other production. The market plays a very active role in our economy and, as a result of the production-waste relationship, it plays a very active role in the environment arena as well.

We realize that there is no way to make the waste from production and consumption and society, in general, go away. However, we can alter the amount, the manner in which it is introduced, and possibly even increase the ecosystem's capacity to absorb or assimilate the waste and, in other ways, affect the pending impact. The problem is not the elimination of waste, but rather our inability to manage or cope with some agreed-upon level. The consensus we must come to is that living assumes some level of waste, and that level, and the mechanism that we employ to cope with it, is what must be agreed upon.

We are at a juncture. We can continue down the path we are on and very certainly we will muddle our way into extinction, or we can embark on a more difficult and unfamiliar path, a path that requires sacrifice and change and compromise. This path in the short term will be littered with the rocks and boulders of controversy, and the consequences of change will require a great amount of sacrifice. If we decide on this route, how do we begin down the path?

In the near term, we cannot simply discard our present societal framework, so we must keep it intact and operational for some time as we work toward more fundamental, ideological changes. Society must deal with the conflicting interests of business, government, environmental groups, and individuals. This understanding is critical: just as environmental problems are linked through a web of interrelationships across the planet, so are the factors of our society. They are inextricably linked with one another and to the environment. The societal dilemma is a question of how and how much, a selection of trade-offs, not just between business and the environmental movement, but also among issues of homelessness, AIDS, drugs, cancer, education and a host of other problems that confront us. This means that we must first acknowledge that the present framework from which we operate as a society has created the bad situation we are in and then decide that we want to change it.

As we do this, we will quickly find solutions for many other related problems. Immediately, and along with this action, we must begin to develop a critical attitude toward our cultural values, science, technology, economic ideals, government and other factors of society so that we can begin to make more fundamental changes for the longer term.

We have the tools and the technology to reverse this trend. The question remains: Do we have the resolve and the commitment? The most often asked question on the ride was, "Can we turn it around?"

My reply was, "Can you?" I am not foolish enough to believe that we have not already caused irreparable harm. At the same time I believe we can significantly reduce the damage, mitigate the long-term impact and restore the ecosystem. I did not cross the United States by myself. I had a lot of help. Cooperation, compromise and the opportunity to become involved were the keys to our successful ride. The same keys can click open the door to our success in today's environmental arena. The opportunity to participate in this issue and the ride was significant to many, and therein lies the answer to the question.

Can we turn it around? We individuals need to continue to believe we can, and somehow cram, jam, stuff, wedge, ram, and squeeze these thoughts and attitudes into our way of life and into the minds of others who are not yet involved. To do this we must provide opportunities for others to become enthusiastic and involved. We must set good examples as environmental concerns begin to occupy what is foremost in our thoughts and become integral to the way we manage our lives. That is the challenge as well as the answer.

On several occasions before the ride, I had a recurring dream. It is the year 2031 and I am in my 70's. I am in a house that is very dark and cold. The lights are on, but it seems very dark. I am reading a book when my grandson walks in. As he comes into the room he enters through some type of vacuum transition chamber. It seems in the dream that each room is purified before someone enters or exits.

My grandson has a magazine with him and he wants to discuss an article with me. A look of concern--maybe anger--marks his face. I notice that the magazine in his hands is TIME, and the article he is pointing to is titled, "We lost the Ecosystem. How?" The article takes us through a chronology of environmental and economic decisions, both bad and good, spanning 80 years. The article states why these decisions were made--economic and political reasons that were fueled by a growing population and a throw-away society.

The article says that in the 1990's the environment became a trendy issue and many actors and actresses became involved. People worked very hard to bring attention to the issue. Several persons walked across the United States, petitions were circulated, and there were sit-ins and protest marches. One person even rode a horse across America. The article then gives a detailed account of all the symptoms of environmental disease that were apparent to everyone--acid rain, global deforestation, ozone depletion, and so on.

My grandson then asks me: "When all of this was going on what were you doing?" and he is angry.

I say: "I rode the horse."

He looks at me, he looks out of the window, and then very slowly he turns back to me and says: "Is that all? Is that it?"

I get up from my chair and walk to the window to look out. There is a crow sitting in a dead tree. It is spring, about 1:00 PM, just after lunch. And it is dark outside.

10

HOW IT ALL BEGAN WAY BACK WHEN: THE ORGANIZATION OF THE RIDE

After several years of research, planning for the ride really began to take shape in late 1988, soon after I attended an Up with People performance at the Al-Marah Arabian ranch in Tucson. Up with People is a very large organization that is made up of many groups of young people who travel around the world as singers, musicians and entertainers in an effort to be, in essence, ambassadors of friendship amongst and between countries. They are not just Americans, but instead the young people come from all over the globe and they bring their message to countries worldwide. They entertain in Russia, the United States, third world and developing countries, as well as in the Middle East and Far East.

My friend, Tracy Church, and I were invited to this performance by her sister's husband, Dale, who is a vice president in the organization. The performance was held in an outdoor show ring. I was very favorably impressed with the facility and asked Tracy and Dale about the owners of the farm, and if they would introduce me to them. We could not find Mrs. Tankersley in time for an introduction, but, as we were leaving, Dale pointed her out in the crowd. Before we left we had a chance to drive around a bit, and this made me realize how enormous the operation truly was.

The ranch is nestled down low along a small stream that comes out of the mountains and, as a result, is hidden from view. It is more than 100 acres and is located in the heart of a growing residential area on the east side of Tucson. It is home to about 450 Arabian horses on a year-round basis. The operation also includes ranches in four other locations in Arizona. We stopped by the main office to pick up some promotional material on the ranch and then left. I told Tracy one week later of my interest in the rainforest and that I had always wanted to ride a horse across the United States. She had not seen this side of me before and was curious: Was I out to lunch or serious?

At the time I was a partner in two businesses, and, since I generally kept personal opinions to myself, to most people I seemed pretty content in Tucson. Inside me, however, there was a growing restlessness.

My partners and I had a small manufacturing and assembly operation in Tucson, with 10 employees, and a much larger operation in Hermosillo, Sonora, Mexico, with about 150 people. Our business involved assembling products for other companies, for example, Laidlaw manufactures drip-dry coat hangers, and, prior to working with us, they manufactured these hangers in Illinois. The wire is cut and twisted to form and then dipped in plastisol and put on a conveyor. The conveyor then carries the coat hangers through an oven that bakes the plastisol. Employees then take the coat hangers off the conveyor and package them in small quantities of six per package, and then in larger boxes of 20 packages to a box, and then one more time in cases of 12 of these twenty-packs. These are then shipped across the border, through customs, and on to stores like K-Mart to be put on a shelf.

I started working in business in 1980 as an Industrial Engineering Analyst with Gates Learjet. It was fun and new. The money was good. I became very successful at it and was eventually promoted to Industrial Engineer. I then left Gates to work for two other companies. One thing led to another and I eventually started my own business in Mexico in 1986.

Before all these developments, I had entered college with aspirations of being an environmental engineer. Like so many in my age group, I caught the tail-end of the environmental movement in the late 60's and early 70's, and then it started to fizzle. I changed my major and got caught up in the business of making money. Let me rephrase that--the business of chasing money. At the time there were no jobs on the environmental horizon, and business was a growing field. For eight years I somehow suppressed my urge to move back into the environmental field. In 1985 I began traveling quite a bit for work. I had the opportunity to see some of the rest of the world. Working in Mexico, Korea, Taiwan, the United Kingdom, and Japan, I found that these countries, like the United States, were abusing natural resources and jeopardizing the world's future.

As time went on I became more and more restless. At first I thought it was the job, so I changed jobs. That wasn't it. I then thought it must be because I was a budding entrepreneur, so I started my own business. It wasn't any of those things. I finally came to the conclusion, late in the game, that I was in the wrong field and that my original aspirations were correct. Now what to do?

Over the next five years I began to informally re-introduce myself at every opportunity to the books, journals, and magazines of the environmental profession. During that period I began, on my own, to prioritize various environmental issues, relying to some extent on my former schooling in botany, biology and chemistry. I came to the conclusion that many others had come to: the world is on some kind of a collision course with the concept of "finite resources," and that the earliest evidence of this is the decline in the world's rainforests. Furthermore, the world is, in fact, a very small place, and we are destroying it bit by bit. Most importantly, I realized that technology is the culprit.

That year, 1987, I told myself I would become involved in the environmental field once again. But how? I had become accustomed to a life-style that was not frivolous, but also not frugal. I could afford what I needed when I needed it and some luxuries to boot. I had also developed a good reputation in my field and a good strong business. I was not sure that I was really willing to give all this up and make the transition.

Or possibly I was experiencing some pre-midlife crisis; I didn't know. You wake up one morning, look in the mirror and say, "Hey, something isn't right." So do you begin to make some changes or do you maintain your life as it is and hope the feeling goes away? As usual, I opted for change and soon after began to contact various colleges. I thought finishing my Master's in Environmental Studies would be a good first step. I settled on Ohio University and the environmental program they have within the Geology Department. Geoff Smith, the head of that program, and I spoke on several occasions from 1985 through 1989. It is now 1990 and I am a student in that program. It took me four years to make the jump. At the age of 32, this is a humbling experience.

When I first started thinking about getting back into the environmental arena, I told myself that it would be best if I would take this one step at a time. I knew that any career transition would require some major financial sacrifices, and I was not sure that, when the time came, I would actually be prepared to do this. So I felt a gradual approach would work best. This would give me the opportunity to back out if I didn't have the guts to go the distance. Sounds pretty "chicken" for a guy that rode a horse across America. But going back to school, as I said before, is a humbling experience.

In my "take it one step at a time" approach, step one was to get involved in the rainforest issue in a more formal way, so I joined several environmental groups and started to go to local meetings. I've always been somewhat impatient with myself and quickly found peripheral involvement was not enough. So, along with my search for a good master's program, I began thinking more and more about the ride. I began to lose interest in my work as I spent more time thinking about the ride and, to some extent, locating information on the routes and previous attempts.

I was in the midst of one of these planning stages when I got the invitation to attend an Up with People performance at the Al-Marah Arabian ranch. The timing could not have been more appropriate. I knew from my research that any attempt at a cross-country ride would have to be well financed and well organized, and to do that I would need credibility and a track record. I needed winners, people who could go the distance and were committed to the event. After returning from the ranch, I spoke with several people about Al-Marah and found the general consensus to be that, if Mrs. Tankersley decided to take on a project, it was as good as done.

When you become involved in an event like this or any other major undertaking, you have to jump in with both feet to pull it off. I knew that, and at this point I was in only half way. I was still working full time on both businesses and torn between my old life-style and this ever-increasing urge to take a jump. Talking with friends about this dilemma was no help. Picture this discussion: Lucian Spataro, entrepreneur and business owner, known in Tucson for his expertise in Mexico, asking friends if he should chuck it all and ride a horse across America. It's not that they did not understand--they just thought I was crazy. The conversations were one-sided and short. I eventually made the decision on my own and in a vacuum. I had very few people to lean on and no one with whom to discuss this. My group of friends thought I was "generally out to lunch" and were more often concerned with the chit-chat at the local bar each Friday after work. After a while that really starts to wear you out. I began to lose touch with everyone but my closest friends, and began to focus more and more on the ride. It began to consume my every waking moment, and this was beginning to isolate me.

In this isolation I made the decision. My thought at the time was: If I can convince Mrs. Tankersley to sponsor the event, we might have something significant here.

I was going to New York for business on September 17, 1988, and was not going to be back in town for about a week. I wanted to set up a meeting with Mrs . Tankersley upon my return, so I put together a brief letter and sent it through Federal Express from my office in Tucson to Al-Marah in Tucson. I probably could have driven the distance and delivered it to her faster. I got a phone call from the Al-Marah marketing director at my office in Tucson four days later. I was still in New York and immediately returned the phone call. The meeting was set.

I first met with the marketing director and then Mrs. Tankersley. I told her of my interest in the rainforest issue and the fact that the ride could bring attention to this cause. I really thought that people along the route and the public in general were not at all familiar with the issue and its implications. I thought A Ride Across America and the attraction people have for horses would help us break the ice and let us introduce the issue. I told her how committed I was and that we could, in fact, make it across with good planning and strong support. The last thing I said to Mrs. Tankersley was that, to do it right and gain the publicity for the issue, people had to believe from the start that we could make it. To convince them, I needed some credibility, and I didn't have any. I told her that the ranch and her commitment and support would give the event the credibility we needed to bring on two environmental groups and several other co-sponsors. She said yes. We were off, not at a full gallop but a fast trot.

My next step was to sign up the two most appropriate environmental groups I could find. I needed strong anchors on both the east and west coasts and preferably in Washington, D.C. I needed a strong lobbying group. I also needed the predominant rainforest group, the Rainforest Action Network (RAN). I went after RAN and the Environmental Policy Institute (EPI). My first call was to RAN and I got through to Randy Hayes, the Executive Director. He thought the idea had some potential, but was not entirely convinced at that time. I offered to send him some material, which he received by Federal Express the next day.

I had a trip scheduled for New York on business the following week, so I thought I could take the opportunity to meet with the people from the Environmental Policy Institute and my Congressman, Jim Kolbe. I could take the Pan Am shuttle down for the afternoon and still make my evening flight. I called the EPI and Congressman Kolbe, and, as luck would have it, both Michael Clark, the Director of EPI, and Jim Kolbe were scheduled to be in D.C. the following week. My intent was to begin developing a board of advisors for the event. On this board I wanted both environmental groups, Congressman Kolbe, and Mrs. Tankersley. From there I could build a good solid board that could help us in several different areas.

The presentation with the Environmental Policy Institute went well. Michael Clark walked out with me afterwards and before leaving said that it was an impressive idea and that he would give it serious thought.

Several weeks later, EPI had a meeting with its board of directors and the idea for the ride came up. Most of the board members were a little concerned about the lack of finances, the safety issue, and the odds whether we could, in fact, make it. When EPI staff member Sharon Benjamin mentioned to the board that Mrs. Tankersley had agreed to support the ride, EPI board member Marie Ridder spoke up and said, "If Bazy is involved, it's on the up and up," or something to that effect (this quote was passed on to me after the meeting by Sharon Benjamin). As a result, the vote to participate went through and I had my first environmental group. I then called Randy Hayes back and asked him to participate as well, and mentioned, in passing, that we had EPI's support. He came on board and we had our two groups. Congressman Kolbe also agreed. That was a very productive trip to D.C.

On the shuttle back I found out that all flights were delayed. Gorbachev was returning from his tour of New York; the result was a major traffic jam, which for some reason slowed air traffic as well. Amazing, I thought, the impact one person can have on a metropolitan area the size of New York--he shut down the whole city. I asked myself. "How are we ever going to ride a horse through here?"

Back in Tucson, we took select board members from each environmental group and combined them into a RIDE ACROSS AMERICA board. We now had some credibility and a very significant list of people to whom I could turn to for help.

At this point I cut back to a half-day at our business and worked from noon till about 4:00 PM. I spent the morning and then late into each evening training and working on the ride. Our training was simply to ride and ride and ride some more. The horses, as well as I, needed to become accustomed to traffic and the daily routine. I rode each day at 4:00 or 5:00 AM, as I would on the ride, until about 10:00 or 11:00 AM. We spent a lot of time on the streets of Tucson during early morning rush-hour traffic.

I saw, on occasion, friends on their way to work at 7:00 AM and those encounters were fairly comical.

"Are you heading for work, Lucian?"

"Yeah, you need a ride?"

I began working on a regular basis on strategy and training with Dr. Cartwright and Dr. Hancock at Al-Marah. As you might guess, this training put a real damper on my social life and, as a result, in the midst of all this my girlfriend, Janine, moved to San Francisco.

In January, 1989, we put together a press conference to kick off the event and started serious training. We invited environmentalist and actor Ted Danson, Mrs. Tankersley, Randy Hayes, and Michael Clark. Mrs. Tankersley offered to hold the press conference in Tucson at Al-Marah. Ted Danson had recently started his own environmental organization, the American Oceans Campaign (AOC), and, through his organization, he was familiar with EPI. EPI invited Ted to attend. He brought the executive director of his newly-formed AOC, Bob Sullnick. EPI's publicity department put together a list of discussion points for Ted Danson and published a news release. In classic Danson style he didn't use the EPI's suggestions but rather spoke of his own thoughts on the issue. He spoke as a person who truly cares, and it was obvious to all that he understood the issues. The media really picked up on this and the event went off very well.

Al-Marah rolled out the red carpet and walked March Along into the room in which the press conference was being held. This really caught the media by surprise, and, in the midst of newspaper reporters and TV cameras, I had my first glimpse of one very important aspect of this ride. In Tucson I could not really plan for my encounters with the media but, instead, I knew I would have to learn (over the distance of the event) how to really understand the media and then communicate, in clear terms, those ideas which I felt were important. This was probably the most difficult problem for me to overcome. So at this first press conference I studied closely how Ted Danson and the others controlled the exchange of information, constantly redefining and focusing what they said so that the outcome--what is read in the papers and heard on the news--was assured. I knew I would have to learn this technique quickly, if we were going to be successful in the media aspect of this event.

After the interviews were over we had a chance to do some riding, and Ted Danson, Bob Sullnick, Randy Hayes and I all took off for a short ride around the ranch. Mrs. Tankersley then hosted a cocktail party at her place that gave us a chance to talk for quite a while. After that, Randy, Michael Clark, and I all went out for a beer. This happened in January. At that time we were all quite excited about the event as it began to gather momentum. I turned over operational control of the business in Tucson to my partner, Joe Tooker, and Luis Lugo took over my work in Mexico.

I was now working full time on the ride and on training. I set up a time table for activities that we needed to complete over the next five months and used this to coordinate with both environmental groups. I had spent all of 1988 laying the groundwork for the route, so all of those contacts were in place and I simply needed to make them aware that the ride was coming. To firm up the route, I needed to get a million-dollar liability policy to the Department of Transportation for each state along the route. With this in hand, the State Department of Transportation would be able to issue a permit to cross the states. Often I had to negotiate with each state to use the road I wanted, and they, in turn, would require that I meet some criteria, for instance, that I have a shadow vehicle, or sometimes that I have no support vehicle. The Department of Transportation often thought that a rider on the side of the road was sometimes less disturbing to traffic than a rider with a slow-moving support vehicle.

In the west only the permit was required, and no vehicle. In the east, states often required that we have a vehicle in high traffic areas and that I avoid rush-hour traffic. Some states allowed horse traffic to actually take precedence over vehicular traffic. In most states, on secondary roads, no permits were required, and, in those states, I rode on through. In the west, however, we were traveling the interstate, which required dozens of permits, it seemed.

Our insurance policy was with Lloyds of London, and we worked with the Equestrian Department of Lloyds and the directing manager, Adrian Pratt, to obtain this policy. We also purchased horse mortality insurance and personal injury insurance of $250,000 for myself and the other team members. Lloyds presented us with a proposal to procure a contingency policy for fund-raising. This was a unique policy and one with which I was not familiar. The concept was like this: We pay Lloyds $19,980 for a policy that will insure us in the event that we do not succeed in raising $1 million. In other words, if we do not raise the money they will pay the difference. I think they were assuming we had some huge fund-raising network behind us and that it was a foregone conclusion we would, in fact, raise the money. In detail and with our lawyer. I went over the policy, which was faxed to me from England; our lawyer was amazed. It seems for $19,980 you can

Press conference with Ted Danson, March Along and Lucian in Tucson at Al-Marah Arabians.
Courtesy of Susan Victoria

guarantee $1 million. I did not feel comfortable taking out the policy, for two reasons: (1) We were not that well funded; true we did have a strong board of advisors and two strong environmental groups behind us, but we still were not doing well in the pre-event fund-raising category; (2) We did not have the cash up-front to buy the policy. In the future, however, if I ever do another event like this, I will take out the contingency policy. I am sure there are several situations in which Lloyds would not have been responsible for payment, but all of those could have been worked out before starting the event. I now know that contingency insurance exists and is important in any major fund-raising effort, because anything that can happen will, and, in this case, did.

On behalf of the ride, Al-Marah sent several letters to clients and friends like Michael Landon and Mrs. William Randolph Hearst, Mrs. Hearst agreed to serve on the board of advisors for the ride and soon thereafter sent a check to help in our fund-raising efforts. Mrs. Tankersley gave me the number for the Hearst Castle in California, so I called to thank Mrs. Hearst. When calling other board members, I would often get a personal secretary or assistant who would forward a message for me. In this case I called and Mrs. Hearst answered the phone; I was not prepared for this. I was, instead, prepared to give my usual spiel, "I'm calling on behalf of the ride and want to thank you for your donation of money and, in this case, time. Could you please pass that message on for me?"

Well, I caught Mrs. Hearst at breakfast and talked with her for about 20 minutes. After that phone call I was really pleased that we were getting this kind of involvement. I thought that we had a very good chance of meeting all of our expectations, primarily to finish the ride and raise a substantial sum of money.

We were looking for a self-enclosed trailer for both people and horses. We found a company in England, called English Coach, that produced just such a vehicle. I called and got a good response from Ian Burns, the head of the United States operation. Initially, Ian agreed to let us use a coach for the event, so I was ecstatic. Several weeks later, I found out that Ian would not be able to let us use the coach and began to hedge on his original agreement. He offered instead to lease a vehicle to us. I was less interested in leasing and more than a little annoyed. On his word I had gone ahead and begun to make arrangements to use the coach, i.e., insurance and gas estimates, etc. I had also told the other board members that we would be using a coach.

Ian called me back to apologize and to say that all of his coaches were going to be used that summer for the great American car race, which lasts about ten days. This all began to make no sense to me, so I told Ian I was not interested in leasing a coach and was more interested in receiving the donation of a coach. With this in mind, he offered to introduce me to several of his clients who for some reason or other were not using their coaches that summer and might be willing to let us use one so the owners could receive the write-off. One of those clients happened to be Sylvestor Stallone. Ian's idea of an introduction was a phone number. I thought, "What the hell," and gave it a shot.

I never actually got to talk with Mr. Stallone but I did talk with everyone else in his organization, including Marcy Brubaker and Susan Persily. They were all good to work with, but, after more than two weeks, the answer was "No." No English Coach. I was devastated. It was instrumental and I had based much of my planning on using a coach.

We still had a couple of other holes to fill. We needed a crew person to handle the horses, a vehicle to take the place of the English coach, and a shadow vehicle as well. We needed an alternative to steel shoes for the horses and we needed more corporate sponsorship. I also needed more help from both environmental groups. The Rainforest Action Network and I were doing most of the work and EPI, was just barely hanging in there with us.

When finalizing details for the ride, I was having a difficult time coordinating with EPI. I proposed that they assign a person to this project and give it a higher priority. I later found out that the organization was in the midst of a major shake-up. EPI had agreed to merge with Friends of the Earth. This, it seems, was a friendly merger and one of necessity. Friends of the Earth needed EPI's fund-raising know how and talent. EPI, on the other hand, could use the name, the international network and large membership provided by Friends of the Earth. Both groups were familiar with one another, as several years earlier they had been one and the same before splitting up. The now reunited and newly-merged organization retained the more well-known name, Friends of the Earth.

I was not privy to this information, however, and, in looking back, the impact of this merger on the ride was considerable. EPI had committed to help, but simply could not organize itself sufficiently in the midst of this merger to make a consistent contribution. Not being aware of the pending merger, in my impatience I began putting more and more pressure on them to get involved. The ride was looming on the horizon and we were getting very little support from EPI. As the merger moved ahead, the project was continually being reassigned. This would require each time that I bring these new people up to date on the status of the ride and various needs we were trying to fill.

Out of frustration, and with no other alternative, RAN and I began carrying the ball, with EPI as a co-sponsor only in name. At this late date I had no alternative other than to move ahead, working with RAN and interfacing very little with EPI. I found out about the merger in April and now at least everything seemed to make a little more sense. I thought: Since the ride was a long event and we were still seven months away from the finish, if RAN and I could carry the ball and get this event off the ground and moving, then EPI or now Friends of the Earth (FOE) could jump in later with some support, two or three months down the road, after things settled out a bit from the merger. This would give them time to restructure and regroup.

Meanwhile, the staff at EPI/FOE were becoming more and more involved in the merger and less accessible. We were moving at such a rapid rate toward the start date that, whenever I did get a chance to speak with EPI/FOE, the updates were completely foreign to them because they were not actively involved in the planning. What I tried to do was lessen their burden in the short term by not tying up their time with details.

This proved to be a bad decision. They became more isolated from the event and this, in combination with the fact that they were day by day becoming more and more involved in the pending merger and their internal problems, led them to some wrong conclusions. The lack of information caused them to become, as an organization often times does, suspicious of our progress, which led to several very emotional phone conversations. I was doing my best to protect those EPI/FOE staff members I was working with by not indicating that they were not helping.

I let this go on too long and then, eventually, in some of the later phone conversations, I began to reveal what was really going on and that we were not receiving much support. This upset the staff with whom I was assigned to work.

One thing led to another and paranoia and further confusion were the result. EPI/FOE flew in an outside consultant named Bob Harvey to give them a third opinion. I spoke with Bob for over six hours in Tucson in April. He gave me a copy of his six-page report on the status of the ride, and I agreed with almost everything he said. I thought the report was extremely accurate.

I was very much surprised when EPI/FOE chose to withdraw from the event. They withdrew in April, six months after they initially agreed to be part of the event, four months after our first press conference, and one month before the start of the ride.

Initially, their withdrawal seemed catastrophic, but, in looking back, it was a blessing in disguise. It allowed us to rally and organize. From that point on, we moved at a much quicker pace. Several of the EPI board members who represented EPI on the RIDE ACROSS AMERICA board stayed on with us. This helped lessen the impact of EPI's official withdrawal and these people, along with the rest of the board members, became instrumental during the event.

EPI/FOE's official stance was that their resources could be better utilized elsewhere on other projects and that the ride was not organized sufficiently to see a maximum return on our effort.

I want to stress an important point about environmental groups in general. They are simply organizations of people with their own problems, just like the corporations and government agencies they battle. They have many agendas like any other organization, and the frustrations experienced by environmental groups rival those of any corporation. They have their own turf to protect and will do so with vigor.

While writing on this somewhat controversial subject I have been torn between saying what I truly feel, voicing my opinion on things that I feel people should know, and, on the other hand, not rocking the boat. I could simply try to get this book into the hands of as many people as I can so they can learn a little about what we did and a little more about the issues we've discussed. I do not feel comfortable, however, eliminating parts of the story just because they may not be pleasant. The societal and environmental problems that confront us today go much deeper than a simple "it's their fault or your fault." It is not an either/or situation, and we can not simply point fingers and say "stop." It is much more complicated than that. The problems that result come from flaws in the framework of society and the decision-making apparatus that we employ. That apparatus is affected by numerous demands and needs. This framework, and the idealogy that underlies our decision-making, demands innovative thinking.

As the poet Wendell Berry once said, *"How superficial and foolish we would be to think that we could correct what is wrong merely by tinkering with the institutional machinery. The changes that are required are fundamental changes in the way we are living."* The organizations that are part of this societal framework include the environmental groups, government agencies, and corporations, and, as a result, you cannot simply point to one or the other and say "Solve the problem" because these various factors of society are inextricably linked to one another much like the different organisms in a ecosystem where an effect on one has an effect on another. Any real and positive change will require unprecedented compromise and cooperation and, in this manner, we will see real progress.

I rode a horse across the United States for an environmental cause, and, in the process, I learned some good things and some bad things about the movement that I was not aware of when I started. If I tell the story, I need to tell the whole story because I think it is important for people to know, and, if this generates a lot of controversy, so be it. That may not be all bad.

I've tried to explain some of the circumstances--for example, in EPI's case they went through the same turmoil any organization might in a merger and the reactions were human reactions. My only complaint is that we suffered and it affected our event.

I hope that the environmental groups are big enough to acknowledge that the movement has its shortcomings, because others are beginning to and this will happen more and more as the movement grows and comes under closer scrutiny. Before the environmental movement can grow substantially in the future, it will need to contend with two inherent and underlying problems: (1) common goals and an over-all strategy and (2) differentiation. Initially you would think that the resolution of both would be difficult, if not impossible. It is essential that we resolve the contradiction. The resolution of these two problems will allow the movement to grow substantially in the future. As previously stated, the top 25 environmental groups have over 13 million members and a combined budget in excess of 1/2 billion dollars annually. If we could focus this nut of credibility, money, and manpower, the movement could be of even greater influence, yet the perception continues that the movement lacks an overall strategy and designated leadership. Among many members of the movement, there is still quite a difference of opinion on both the overall direction and the approach to be taken.

This lack of consensus is an underlying problem that will continue to plague the movement and hinder its effectiveness and growth. This coupled with competition among various environmental groups for funding creates a situation in which conflict of interest questions are present. One example might be a situation when two or more environmental groups pursue funding with XYZ corporation. After several months of lobbying, one receives funding and the other does not. This raises the question, What did our environmental group commit to do over and above what the other group had proposed? The concern is that some environmental groups may commit to do more than others. We want an attitude like that of Thomas Exton, fund-raiser for the environmental movement who in the past has said, "When they say the money's tainted, I say, taint enough." Where do we draw the conflict of interest line and who draws it? This, like the lack of consensus, will continue to undermine the credibility of the movement and to slow its progress and growth. These two very important issues will need to be resolved short term to allow the movement to realize its full potential.

One of our big concerns was funding. With two months left to go, we were short on cash. We needed $48,000 to complete the event, and we had commitments for about half of that. The Rainforest Action Network was confident enough and committed enough to carry us for the balance. Randy Hayes was instrumental; he was utterly committed, which did a lot for our morale. The railroad companies that EPI had been courting fell through. So did J/B Whiskey, with which EPI had had a problem. EPI's concern was that the event might not be looked upon in a favorable manner with an alcohol co-sponsor. I was willing, but the project fell through. J/B eventually went with a promotion that played off the drought they were experiencing in New York. I think it went something like "When it rains it pours J/B" or something to that effect. Chevron came through with an educational grant to RAN on behalf of RAN's educational efforts, one of which that summer was the ride. I spoke off and on with Audrey Goins at Chevron about our event, our goals, and our objectives. In June we found that the grant had come through. By May we had enough in the kitty to get the ride off the ground. Our efforts along the way would raise the balance.

We were still having some problems determining which saddle we were going to use and, if, in fact, we would need to switch to Easy Boots and when. I was a little concerned with our ability to accomplish the task of caring for the horses' feet on the road or in the middle of the desert and who we would use as a farrier if we needed one. We knew from experience that our first set of steel shoes would take us to Arizona and hopefully all the way to Flagstaff. In Flagstaff we knew people who could point us to a farrier we could trust with Willy's feet. As a back-up to Easy Boots I began putting together a list of farriers in towns along our route. I would call a veterinarian in XYZ town and ask him/her which local farriers would be the most qualified; in this manner I assembled a good list of farriers that we could tap into if need be. The strategy we settler on was to ride using the steel shoes and Easy Boots for the balance of the ride.

The choice of a saddle and riding gear was not as easy a decision to come to and took some experimentation. We started the ride with the EPIC Endurance saddle, endurance stirrups, a cantle bag, a pommel bag, a saddle pad and a saddle blanket, a water bottle, lead rope, stethoscope, a watch and flashlight. As the ride wore on, I began to jettison much of this equipment, and changed saddle and blanket combinations, often in an attempt to find the most appropriate combination. Through trial and error we eventually ended up with a single wool blanket, a Porter endurance saddle, a water bottle and collapsible water bucket, a cantle bag and a pommel bag. The larger and heavier Porter saddle was much better at distributing my weight over the horse's back. I kept the endurance stirrups when I made a saddle switch. These stirrups were instrumental in allowing me to ride the distances I did each day. These stirrups are much wider than a normal stirrup and average about 3 inches front to rear. They are padded and much more comfortable and practical than narrow stirrups. Much of the gear we eventually settled on was supplied to us by Patty Phelan as a donation from her company's catalog.

To solve our problem we chose to go with Easy Boots and had the inventor, Neel Glass, and his wife, Lucille, fit the horses personally. These boots were high-impact rubber boots with clamps that fit over the horses steel shoes, and they last over 800 miles, or 4 weeks, two or three times what the steel shoes were lasting. We still used the steel shoes and put these boots over them, so the hooves had time to grow. Also, if the horse should throw an Easy Boot, we would still have the steel shoes to ride on that day. In that case, I would have to take off all of the Easy Boots so the horse could walk evenly on all four steel shoes. In camp we would put all of the Easy Boots on again for the ride the next day.

Regarding the route itself, from a logistics standpoint I would say that the first 175 miles in California, from Huntington Beach on up into the high desert, the Indian reservation in Arizona, the Missouri stretch, the West Virginia stretch and the last 75 miles on the east coast were the most difficult. We had to ad lib quite a bit, changing our route here and there as we discovered road closures, construction, traffic, high

168

temperatures, fences, or no place to camp. From a physical and mental standpoint, the stretch along the Colorado River was miserable. The stretch from Flagstaff and on across the Indian reservation (this area is called the Painted Desert) was also very difficult as we were riding in the midst of this area's hottest season. Last, but most important, was the stretch from Albuquerque to Joplin. Mentally this was the tightest stretch; all I could see in the distance was horizon upon horizon that seemed to go on and on and on. To ride a horse from coast to coast as we did, from knee-deep in saltwater on one coast to knee-deep in saltwater on the other coast, will be very difficult in the years to come. As the population base continues moving from the Midwest to the East and West Coastal Regions, these areas will become more and more congested. Currently they are a maze of super highways and small communities with fences everywhere. In a ride like this, fences were a major frustration and I spent many hours riding up and down fence-lines in an attempt to find a way through.

Many people ask me how I chose the route. My first concern was time and weather, and my second concern was media exposure. I wanted the shortest path possible that would present us with the greatest opportunity to talk with people about this issue. I took out a map of the United States and a string, and I located the two largest cities, Los Angeles and New York, and laid the string down on the map in a straight line from L.A. to New York. I then taped the string to the map and stuck it on the wall. That was my route.

Further calculations showed that the straight route, as the crow flies along the string, was about 2200 miles using the legend on the map. I knew I could not ride right along the string because in many places there were no roads. We needed water and feed, and we needed to make good time. I knew from experience that it was much faster riding along a road than bushwhacking across the desert or some other wilderness area. With this in mind, and using many local and regional topographical maps I then found all of the roads, highways, and trails parallel with this string. Staying as close to the string as I could, I simply highlighted these routes, connecting super highways with power lines and then secondary roads, and so on until I had my own route along that string.

The route ended up being a mish-mash of roads, highways, power lines, railroad rights-of-way and ad libbing. This route meandered north and south of the string, adding about 800 miles to the route, but generally we tried to stay as close to that string as we possibly could. I then calculated the distance and our pace, located the various metropolitan areas along the route, and began working with Francesca at RAN to schedule media events and fund-raisers. I obtained the permits in the same manner, systematically working with each state along the master route until we had three folders full of permits and letters of approval for specific routes.

We were still looking for a crew person or persons to work the ride.

Al-Marah had agreed to supply the crew. It was an extremely difficult position to fill. The crew persons had to have horse-sense, be committed to go the distance and have a vested interest in doing so, and be able to withstand the physical rigors of the ride. In addition, our crew members would have to be articulate enough to communicate with the media on both horse-related subjects and the rainforest issue. This caliber of persons typically would be employed in the equine industry full-time and would not be able to shake loose for five months to a ride across America. Even so, we found our crew--Sheryl Studley and Brad and Joyce Braden.

As we hit New Mexico, we needed additional support and we added Bob and Bea Shepard to the team. Just as we were firming up our crew, the Jim Click Ford Agency in Tucson offered to supply a truck to pull the trailer/house that we had located for the ride. We now had our vehicle situation under control and our crew.

We were in pretty good shape, though still having some problems in establishing the fund-raising format for the event. Our corporate approach was not working, so we shifted gears and decided to go after individuals along the route and at each fund-raiser. Our objectives, once again, were to 1) finish the ride, 2) educate and expose as many people to the cause as we could along the way, and 3) raise money. At our start on May 19th we were looking pretty good on objectives one and two, but still needed to do more work on three.

As we were leaving Tucson on our way over to L.A., we thought we could focus on raising money as we rode along the route, and, in fact, that is what we did. Our goals, as we stated before, were to finish the ride and bring this issue into the hearts of as many as we could along the way and raise money for this cause. Somehow over the last eight months our priorities had been reversed, reinterpreted and influenced so that money had somehow become the predominant and primary goal and, from the onset, it was not our intent that it should be. With this in mind we went about reestablishing our goals in order of priority and, through this exercise, it became very apparent that we could and should concentrate on our primary goals and, via success in this area, the rest would ultimately come.

This ride was both an endurance event and a media event. These two goals were not congruent with one another at all times and this made the actual riding and the planning for this event difficult. Often we were torn between riding farther on a particular day or altering our route to make a media commitment. Our need to meet both our media commitments and our ride goals was an on-going cause for concern and controversy among team members and others as well. On one hand, I would suggest to anyone else who might be inclined to break this record that they focus primarily on the ride and not use the event as a way to attract attention to a specific issue. Even though it is an excellent way of doing just that it will sap your energy and slow you down. On the other hand, I thought when I first began the ride that our team could make the crossing in four months. I now believe that a team in that time-frame using three horses and one rider would need to rest a week for every month of riding which is what we essentially did without knowing that we needed to or planning to do this. I believe in looking back that our short rests along the way were essential and that the media commitments helped break the routine which led to a much needed injection of energy and enthusiasm.

This was a very long and physically rigorous event, and for me the purpose of the event--to bring attention to the rainforest issue--was significant as a motivational force. If it were not for this purpose, I might have stopped on numerous occasions. At various times the multiple goals helped, but in some cases having two reasons for completing this event was a cause of many problems; however, in the overall scheme of things this may have been the real reason we actually finished. I do not know if a team with one goal, that of setting the record, could maintain the desire and focus for that time frame and still shave a couple of days off our record. For me if there were not some larger purpose in mind, I probably would have quit. Apparently our approach was right if our intent was to bring attention to some specific issue as we did, but if our goal were simply to set a record, our approach may or may not have been the most expedient. It really depends on what kind of person you are and what motivates you to do the things you do. It worked for me.

This is the READER'S DIGEST version of the planning and significant events behind the ride. There are many more activities that took place and countless other details that we had to contend with, but, by and large, these were the most significant.

For further information on the Rainforest and other Rainforest related projects you may wish to contact the following:

The Jane Goodall Institute
P.O. Box 41720
Tucson, AZ 85717
(602) 325 1211

Rainforest Action Network
301 Broadway, Suite A
San Francisco, CA 94133
(415) 398 4404